From Ice Cream to the Internet

Using Franchising to Drive the Growth and Profits of Your Company

From Ice Cream to the Internet

Using Franchising to Drive the Growth and Profits of Your Company

Scott A. Shane
Department of Economics
Weatherhead School of Management
Case Western Reserve University

PEARSON
Prentice
Hall

Library of Congress Number: 2004111943

Publisher: Tim Moore
Executive Editor: Jim Boyd
Editorial Assistant: Richard Winkler
Development Editor: Russ Hall
Marketing Manager: Martin Litkowski
International Marketing Manager: Tim Galligan
Cover Designer: Chuti Prasertsith
Managing Editor: Gina Kanouse
Senior Project Editor: Kristy Hart
Copy Editor: Krista Hansing
Senior Indexer: Cheryl Lenser
Senior Compositor: Gloria Schurick
Manufacturing Buyer: Dan Uhrig

© 2005 by Pearson Education, Inc.
Publishing as Prentice Hall
Upper Saddle River, New Jersey 07458

Prentice Hall offers excellent discounts on this book when ordered in quantity for bulk purchases or special sales. For more information, please contact U.S. Corporate and Government Sales, 1-800-382-3419, corpsales@pearsontechgroup.com. For sales outside the U.S., please contact International Sales at international@pearsoned.com.

Printed in the United States of America

First Printing

ISBN 0-13-149421-X

Pearson Education LTD.
Pearson Education Australia PTY, Limited.
Pearson Education Singapore, Pte. Ltd.
Pearson Education North Asia, Ltd.
Pearson Education Canada, Ltd.
Pearson Educatión de Mexico, S.A. de C.V.
Pearson Education—Japan
Pearson Education Malaysia, Pte. Ltd.

To Lynne, for supporting my writing
and everything else that I do

CONTENTS AT A GLANCE

ACKNOWLEDGMENTS

I decided to write this book after having researched franchising for more than a decade as a faculty member at Georgia Tech, MIT, the University of Maryland, and Case Western Reserve University. My research on designing the right strategy and structure to make franchise systems successful seemed to hit a chord with entrepreneurs and managers. Several of my studies were discussed in popular publications such as the *New York Times*, *The Wall Street Journal*, and *Entrepreneur Magazine*. I appeared on several radio and television programs to talk about franchising. This, of course, led many prospective and current franchisors to contact me and ask me to serve as a consultant to their businesses.

What I discovered from this consulting experience surprised me. The basic principles about how to design effective franchise systems that academic researchers had known for years and had shown convincingly in scholarly articles were virtually unknown among practitioners of franchising. For instance, academic research offered strong evidence about how to decide on the right royalty rate for a franchise system, based on a variety of factors, including such things as the support services the franchisor would provide, the margins in the business, the value of the franchisor's trade name, and the nature of the franchisor's industry. Yet franchisors would tell me that they selected their royalty rate because "the number had a nice ring to it" or "because it was a round number." Of course, the fact that these people were then coming to me for advice, saying that their royalty rate was too low and that they could not make a profit, suggested that they could use the information generated from academic research—if only they could get access to it in an understandable form.

When I looked around for things to show my clients, I realized that there were no good books or articles to give people to read. Giving people original academic articles in dense prose, with mathematical formulas, complex data analysis, and arcane theory, was not an option. Yet no book or set of articles summarized all that we knew about how to set up an effective and profitable franchise system in a simple and straightforward way that would give them the key pieces of information that they needed to be successful. All the books and articles that I could find written in a language that normal people could understand either focused on buying a franchise from the perspective of a franchisee or offered the personal perspective of a franchisor or franchise attorney, much of it based on pretty dubious evidence. So I decided to write this book.

Many people's influence was important in writing this book. First of all, I would like to thank all of the managers, entrepreneurs, and newspaper and magazine reporters who forced me to translate what I knew from my academic research about franchising into simple and straightforward principles that people can use to create successful franchise systems.

I would also like to thank all of the scholars and practitioners on whose work I have drawn to provide the framework for this book. Although the ideas presented in this book were influenced by many people, several are particularly important: Jeffrey Bradach, Jim Brickley, Rajiv Dant, Erik Gordon, Francine Lafontaine, and Patrick Kaufmann. The articles that these people wrote were extremely valuable in helping me to develop the ideas presented in this book.

Over the years, a variety of collaborators have taught me a great deal about franchising. In particular, Maw-Der Foo, Venky Shankar, and Chester Spell stand out. Other colleagues have generously given their time to discuss franchising with me, thereby shaping many of the ideas in this book; these include Susan Athey, Simon Johnson, and Scott Stern. I would like to thank all of them. This book would not have been possible without the help of these people.

I would also like to thank my editor, Jim Boyd. Not only did Jim believe in the vision that I had of turning ideas developed by academics and thoughtful practitioners into a practical book to help people be more successful at franchising their businesses, but he was instrumental in shaping that vision. His efforts to help me craft the right type of book, providing enough explanation and examples to educate readers without being too academic, were invaluable.

Finally, I would like to thank my wife, Lynne, my daughter, Hannah, and my son, Ryan. Each of them helped me in their own ways. Hannah helped me by being my source of joy and inspiration (as well as an excellent playmate when I needed breaks from writing). Ryan helped me by being such a good baby that I could get this book written and revised. Lynne helped me by always being willing to discuss my work and give me feedback on it, as well as encouraging me and supporting me in my efforts.

ABOUT THE AUTHOR

Dr. Scott A. Shane is Professor of Economics and Entrepreneurship at the Weatherhead School of Management at Case Western Reserve University. The author of numerous scholarly articles on franchising, Dr. Shane has consulted with many current and potential franchisors on the topics outlined in this book. Dr. Shane has also written or edited seven other business books including: *Finding Fertile Ground: Identifying Extraordinary Opportunities for New Ventures; Academic Entrepreneurship: University Spinoffs and Wealth Creation; A General Theory of Entrepreneurship: The Individual-Opportunity Nexus; Entrepreneurship: A Process Perspective;* and *Foundations of Entrepreneurship.* Dr. Shane holds a Ph.D. from The Wharton School, University of Pennsylvania.

INTRODUCTION

Franchising has become the dominant mode of retail entrepreneurship in the United States. The number of businesses involved in franchising in some way is astounding. At most recent count, almost 2,300 companies manage franchise chains in more than 80 industries. These companies work with 767,000 franchisees that employ 10 million people—as many as all manufacturers of durable goods combined.[1] Moreover, franchise systems generate $1 trillion in sales annually, accounting for approximately 40 percent of all U.S. retail sales.[2]

Franchising is also becoming a more common business model. The number of franchised outlets in the United States increased by 146 percent from 1980 to 2003, an average of 6 percent per year, as franchises have replaced independent businesses in industries as diverse as fast food, banking, Internet services, automotive repair, and eye care. In fact, in the United States today, a new franchised outlet opens approximately every 8 minutes.

This pace of growth has been on an accelerating trajectory in recent years. The number of franchised outlets in the U.S. economy grew by only 28 percent in the 11 years between 1980 and 1991, but it grew 92 percent in the 11 years between 1991 and 2002.[3]

Franchising is growing even faster internationally, leading the House Committee on Small Business to define franchising as one of America's most rapidly growing exports. Currently, approximately 500 American companies operate more than 50,000 franchised outlets overseas. Ninety percent of all franchisors in this country are planning to expand internationally in the next decade, and roughly half of all franchised outlets established in the past decade were set up outside the United States.

The industry distribution of franchising is also quite broad. Franchise systems are currently found in more than 80 different industries, with more industries being added every year. Recent industry additions to franchising include advertising for on-hold telephone calls and outlets offering three-dimensional ultrasound, allowing people to see their soon-to-be-born children.

Despite the common perception that it is all about small business, franchising is a strategy adopted by a surprisingly large number of big businesses. Several Fortune 500 companies, including Ashland Oil, First Interstate Bancorp, McDonald's®, Medicine Shoppes International, Merrill Lynch, Ponderosa®, Postal Instant Press, Prudential Insurance, S.C. Johnson, Shoney's®, Snelling and Snelling, TCBY Enterprises, Union Carbide, and Wendy's International, have used or currently use franchising as a business model.[4] Five percent of all franchisors are public companies, including Ben Franklin® stores, Big O Tires®, Doubletree® Hotels, Gymboree®, Microage Computer Centers, Staff Builders® International, and Swisher International.[5] Ironically, franchising is also an avenue for private equity firms interested in taking public companies private again, as well as financing management buyouts and making acquisitions. Recent private equity deals involving franchising include The Dwyer

Group, Cottman® Transmission Systems, Carvel® Ice Cream, Sylvan Learning Centers®, El Pollo Loco®, Chem-Dry®, Meineke® Car Care, Ruth's Chris® Steakhouse, Nutri Magic®, and Money Mailer® Systems.[6]

The Purpose of This Book

Obviously, franchising is an important business model chosen by some firms in some industries. What makes franchising particularly interesting, however, is that the adoption of it appears to be a strategic choice made by some businesses and not others. For example, although at least 12 coffee companies franchise, Starbucks® steadfastly resists the use of this strategy. As a result, many franchised coffee companies, such as Seattle's Best Coffee®, compete head to head with a giant chain of company-owned coffee houses. Similarly, although most large restaurant firms franchise their operations—in the restaurant industry, only 13 of the 100 largest chains chose not to franchise—General Mills operates its Olive Garden® and Red Lobster® chains directly.[7] This leads General Mills to compete as a company-owned chain with many other firms that use a very different approach to operate their businesses.

The choice of some companies to compete by franchising and other companies to compete by owning all of their own outlets leads to the first goal of this book: to explain when franchising is a good strategy for a firm to adopt and when it is not. Franchising has advantages and disadvantages that influence the ways in which firms compete successfully with each other. As the entrepreneur who founded a company or a manager who runs one, you need to decide how to best compete with firms that franchise when you do not, and vice versa.

In addition, you probably want to figure out whether you are better off using franchising in your business. The chapters that follow will help you to answer this question: Should I franchise my business or not? This book examines the feasibility of franchising in your industry, the pros and cons of franchising, the legal and institutional requirements to franchise, and the management challenges of doing so, to help you to understand whether your company is better off on balance being a franchisor.

Of course, you might have already decided that you should franchise your business (or reading the first few chapters has led you to decide to adopt this business model). As you certainly realize, being successful at franchising requires you to design an effective franchise system. This book will also help you to do that, identifying the policies and strategies that are necessary to create a winning franchise operation.

This is important because, despite the widespread reach of franchising, surprisingly few companies succeed at franchising. In fact, of the more than 200 new franchise systems established in the United States each year, 25 percent don't even make it to their first anniversary, approximately three quarters fail within a decade, and only 15 percent make it to 17 years. The poor performance of most firms that franchise raises several questions that you need to answer: Why do so many new franchisors fail? What do successful franchisors do differently from unsuccessful franchisors? This book examines the policies and strategies that successful franchisors adopt and how they differ from those of unsuccessful franchisors, to provide a framework for entrepreneurs and managers to understand how to establish a winning franchise system. This book also serves as a guide for entrepreneurs and managers with ineffective systems to redesign their systems for success.

How Is This Book Different from Other Books?

Other people have written books about franchising, so it is important for you to know how this book is different from other books on franchising. Perhaps most important, this book takes the perspective of the franchisor, not the franchisee, which is the perspective taken by the vast majority of books on franchising. The franchisee-focused approach is not very useful to managers and entrepreneurs trying to figure out how to make their companies successful at franchising. Books that take this focus concentrate on what an individual should do to get started as a franchisee and seek to answer questions like "How do I select the right franchise outlet to buy?" or "What are the hot properties in franchising today?" They offer little guidance to managers and entrepreneurs about how to grow their companies through franchising or how to use franchising as a strategy to make their companies more profitable. In contrast, this book provides a guide for entrepreneurs and managers to use in evaluating franchising as a business strategy.

This book is also different from most books on franchising, which focus on the operational details of *how* to franchise. While "how to" books are important and are fine for answering many questions that are important to franchisors, such as "How do I advertise my franchise at a trade show?" or "How do I fill out a Uniform Franchise Offering Circular (UFOC)?", they do very little to help entrepreneurs and managers succeed. Unfortunately, there is no answer to a "how to" question that is a secret to success. Insight into success tends to come from answers to "why" questions. So there is no way to follow the recommendations of "how-to" books to increase the chances of being successful with franchising.

To be successful in franchising, you need to master the basic principles of business and economics that underlie franchising. What you need is a book that tells you what those principles are and how to apply them to design an effective franchise system. This book provides those principles and helps you use them to design an effective franchise operation.

Moreover, this book takes the idea of identifying these principles—and explaining how to apply them—seriously by developing a framework of rules for success that are based on rigorous academic research. This framework explains why certain actions should lead to success and offers persuasive evidence to support those explanations. The book uses this framework of research to identify decision rules for whether franchising is appropriate for your industry, whether the benefits of franchising outweigh the costs, whether you have a business concept that is appropriate for franchising, and which policies and strategies to adopt to make franchising successful. The decision rules presented in the chapters that follow will help you to choose such things as the right royalty rate and franchise fee for your franchise system; whether to use master franchising, area development agreements, or sub-franchising to grow your system; and what policies to adopt to control the behavior and actions of your franchisees.

What This Book Does Not Do

Having said what this book does, it is only fair to tell you what it doesn't do. This book doesn't deal with the day-to-day management of a franchise system. It doesn't tell you how to accomplish the nitty-gritty steps that are necessary to set up a franchise system. Many books out there can explain these things to you. In addition, there is a cottage industry of franchise consultants and attorneys whose bread and butter lies in offering this assistance. It is certainly helpful for you to read other books on franchising or to talk to franchise attorneys and consultants—in fact, it is probably a very bad idea to begin franchising without having first talked to a franchise attorney. However, the information that these experts provide is not a substitute for what is contained here. You need to develop a good, sound analysis of whether to franchise your business, how to compete with firms that do not franchise if you do (and vice versa), and what kinds of policies and strategies you need to adopt if you decide to franchise. The lessons contained in the chapters that follow will help you do just that.

Who Should Read This Book and When Should They Read It?

You should read this book if you are thinking of starting to franchise your business, whether you are an entrepreneur or a manager in an existing company. It will help you to figure out whether franchising is a good strategy for your company, as well as the right policies and strategies to adopt if you choose to franchise. You should also read this book if you already operate a franchise system, but your system is not doing well. You are likely to find tips here that you can use to improve your existing franchise operations. You should also read this book even if you are not planning to franchise your business, but your competitors are. It will provide useful information for you about the weaknesses of franchising as a competitive strategy that you might be able to exploit. Furthermore, you should read this book if you are thinking of becoming a franchisee or are already one. Although this book approaches franchising from the franchisor's perspective, it is useful for you to know what franchisors do and why they do it. That knowledge will help ensure that your relationship with your franchisor is as free of conflict as possible.

Ideally, you should read this book when you begin thinking about franchising. Because this book focuses on identifying the favorable industries for franchising, the right business concepts for franchising, the pros and cons of the business model, and the policies and strategies that make franchising effective, the tools and ideas that you will get from reading the book are best used before you are locked into a particular approach. The frameworks described in the following pages, along with the recommendations for "dos and don'ts" and the questions to ask yourself, are designed to help you think about whether to franchise and how to set up a successful franchise system if you decide to do so.

However, even if you have an existing franchise system that might be difficult to change, or you have adopted a strategy of not franchising while your competitors have adopted one of franchising, it is not too late to read this book. Many things in the chapters that follow are valuable to entrepreneurs and managers even after a franchise system is in operation.

Sources of Knowledge Underlying This Book

Because I have said that this book uses academic research to create a framework for deciding whether to franchise and for designing a successful franchise system if you decide to franchise, it is only fair for me to describe for you the sources of information underlying the book. The book has two specific sources of information. Some parts of the framework and evidence presented here are based on my own primary research. For the past decade, I have researched franchising from the point of view of franchisors. The studies I have conducted provide many useful results for determining whether to adopt policies such as allowing passive ownership of franchised outlets or deciding when to expand your franchise system overseas.

Other parts of the book are based on the research of other academics. I have distilled the key action steps from hundreds of studies that you, as a franchisor, should follow to enhance your performance at franchising.

Regardless of the source, this book compiles, combines, and translates into plain English, material that is otherwise available only in a variety of different academic articles and books. As a result, you will find all of the key concepts that you need to figure out whether to franchise your business; how to compete with companies that franchise if you do not; and how to operate a successful franchise system; summarized and explained in one place, in a clear and straightforward manner.

The Key Lessons

Successful franchisors approach franchising differently from other firms, not because their people are smarter than or different than those in other firms, but because they have learned when, why, and how franchising is successful. This book presents 11 rules to follow for a company to be successful at franchising. Each of these rules is explained in a different chapter of the book:

1. Select the right industry.

2. Understand the advantages of franchising.

3. Pay attention to the disadvantages of franchising.

4. Make sure that your business concept can be franchised.

5. Adopt the right policies to manage the franchise system.

6. Find the right approach to franchisee support and assistance.

7. Develop the right strategy toward franchisee territories.

8. Price the franchises appropriately.

9. Develop the right strategy toward system expansion.

10. Understand the legal and institutional environment of franchising.

11. Recruit, select, and manage franchisees effectively.

An Overview of Chapters

The first rule of franchising explained in this book is to make sure that your industry is one that is appropriate for franchising. Some industries are simply better than other industries for the creation of franchise systems. Half of all franchisors are concentrated in the top ten industries for franchising. In some industries, such as tax preparation, printing and copying, and specialty food retailing, franchisors now account for the majority of all firms.[8] Chapter 1, "Is Franchising Right for Your Industry?", defines franchising and gives a short history of the business model. It then identifies nine characteristics that make franchising appropriate for an industry: Production and distribution occur in limited geographic markets; physical locations are helpful to serving customers; local market knowledge is important to performance; local management discretion is beneficial; brand name reputation is a valuable competitive advantage; the level of standardization and codification of the process of creating and delivering the product or service is high; the operation is labor intensive; outlets are not terribly costly or risky to establish; and the effort of outlet operators is hard to measure relative to their performance.

The second rule of franchising is to understand the advantages offered by this business model. Franchising is not a panacea for all business woes, but it does provide distinct advantages to the firms that use it. Chapter 2, "The Advantages of Franchising," outlines three categories of benefits that franchising provides to firms. It offers an effective model for selecting and providing incentives to outlet operators; an efficient mechanism for obtaining capital and human resources for rapid firm growth; and a lucrative economic model, generating financial returns at relatively low risk.

The third rule of franchising is to understand the drawbacks of this organizational arrangement. The advantages of franchising described in Chapter 2 come at the expense of four major disadvantages, which are discussed in Chapter 3, "The Disadvantages of Franchising":

- Franchisors and franchisees have different goals, which come into conflict.

- Franchisors' use of contracts to link themselves to legally independent franchisees leads to transaction cost problems, such as free riding, which do not exist with company-owned chains.

- Innovation and change initiated at headquarters are more difficult to implement with franchising than with company ownership of outlets.

- The absolute level of profits from franchising is lower than that of operating company-owned outlets.

Making the decision to franchise, figuring out how to compete with firms that do not franchise, and developing the right policies and strategies toward franchising all require an understanding of the four types of disadvantages that franchising entails.

The fourth rule of franchising is to ensure that you have a business concept that is appropriate for franchising. Although many business concepts are valuable, only a small number of them can be franchised to other people. Chapter 4, "What Business Concepts Can Be Franchised?", discusses three categories of factors that make a business concept appropriate for franchising. A business needs to have a valuable system for serving end customers that can bear the additional costs of the franchising structure. Its operations must be composed of a set of procedures that can be written down and taught to others with limited knowledge of the business. Furthermore, the business needs to appeal to enough potential buyers of the concept to make investing in the up-front costs of setting up a franchise system, which can be several hundred thousand dollars, worthwhile.

The fifth rule of franchising is to adopt the right policies to manage a franchise system effectively. Because franchising is a business based on contracts between legally independent companies, franchise systems need fundamentally different policies from company-owned chains. Chapter 5, "Key Franchising Policies," identifies four categories of policies that are necessary for effective franchising:

- Policies to ensure owner operation of outlets.

- Rules for controlling franchisee behavior.

- Policies for setting the correct contract term.

- Rules about franchisee advertising.

To franchise effectively, you need to adopt the right policies in each of these areas. And if you choose not to adopt franchising but you compete with firms that do, you will need to identify the right policies in each of the areas to determine the weaknesses of your competitors' strategies.

The sixth rule of franchising is to ensure that you offer the right level of support and assistance to your franchisees—things such as training, site selection, and purchasing. If you offer too little support to them, you are likely to have trouble attracting franchisees. But if you offer too much support, you are likely to attract the wrong type of franchisees, and do so at a cost that undermines your profitability. Chapter 6, "Franchisee Support and Assistance," discusses four categories of support and assistance that you need to consider offering to your franchisees: training, support services, real estate assistance, and financing. This chapter helps you to figure out the right amount and types of this support to offer at different stages in the life of your franchise system.

The seventh rule of franchising is to develop an effective territorial strategy. Franchising tends to occur in businesses in which sales growth requires the establishment of additional outlets at new locations rather than the expansion of production at an existing location. As a result, it requires franchisors to have a strategy for the establishment of new locations or territories. Often franchisors turn a winning franchise system into a losing one by adopting the wrong territorial strategy. Chapter 7, "Territorial Strategies," identifies the key considerations that you need to make in determining your territorial strategy. It discusses when and how you should use multiunit franchising arrangements, such as master franchising and subfranchising, to exploit new territories, and when you want to offer only single units to prospective franchisees. The chapter also discusses when you want to offer existing franchisees the rights to expand in their territories and when you do not want to use this strategy. Finally, the chapter discusses when you want to establish exclusive territories for your franchisees and how large those territories should be.

The eighth rule of franchising is to price the franchise system correctly. When you become a franchisor, you enter into the business of selling business opportunities. Like anything else, the ability to sell a business opportunity depends on pricing it right. Charge too high a price, and you will not attract franchisees. Charge too low a price, and you will not make a profit. Chapter 8, "Pricing Franchises," discusses the factors that influence the two major components of the price of a franchise: the up-front franchise fee and the ongoing royalties that franchisees pay to franchisors. The chapter also explains how franchise fees and royalty rates should change as your franchise system matures and grows.

The ninth rule of franchising is to develop an effective expansion strategy. Most of the time, franchisors are unsuccessful unless they expand their systems from their initial starting point to the minimum efficient scale of operations for companies in their industries. However, as Chapter 9, "Expansion Strategies," explains, expanding a franchise system successfully involves making the right strategic decisions about when you should begin to franchise your business and the geographical pattern your expansion should take, including its international expansion. The chapter also explains that successful expansion involves operating some company-owned outlets. Therefore you to need to determine the right balance between company-owned and franchised outlets in your system over time, as well as decide which outlets to franchise and which to own.

The tenth rule of franchising is to understand the legal and institutional environment in which it operates. Franchising is a legally regulated mode of doing business, making it important for you to understand how federal and state laws affect the operation of a franchise system. As Chapter 10, "The Legal and Institutional Environment for

Franchising," explains, since 1979, franchisors have had to adhere to rules requiring them to disclose to prospective franchisees standard information about the franchise system and its principals, in a form set forth by the Federal Trade Commission. The chapter also explains that some states have adopted franchise registration and relationship laws that affect how you do business as a franchisor in those states, as well as the right strategy to adopt for franchising in different states. Chapter 10 also discusses the importance of certification of franchise operations by the media and the franchise trade association, the International Franchise Association.

The eleventh rule of franchising is to recruit, select, and manage franchisees effectively. You will not succeed as a franchisor unless you can attract potential franchisees, select the best candidates from among the pool of applicants, and manage them effectively. However, the processes of recruiting, selecting, and managing franchisees are not easy to accomplish effectively. Chapter 11, "Recruiting, Selecting, and Managing Franchisees," provides guidance on how to recruit franchisees successfully by explaining why people buy franchises and how to create a professional sales force that knows ways to generate, qualify, and sell franchise systems to prospects. The chapter also identifies effective selection criteria for ensuring that you choose the best franchisees for your system. Finally, the chapter offers guidance on four basic activities that make managing franchisees more effective: minimizing the number of sources of goal conflict with franchisees; ensuring that the franchise system provides financial benefit to franchisees; communicating clearly about the obligations of franchisees; and controlling franchisee behavior carefully.

The conclusion of the book returns to the theme introduced in the introduction about how to develop an effective franchising strategy. Specifically, it summarizes the key actions that you should take to determine whether to franchise, to compete with firms in your industry that do, and to design the right policies and strategies toward franchising, if that is the mode of business that you opt to use.

1

Is Franchising Right for Your Industry?

Today franchising occurs in more than 80 different industries. Included among them are automobile repair, automobile sales, book selling, building materials, business services, camera sales, car washes, carpet sales, check cashing, computer training, credit agencies, data processing, dentistry, drug stores, dry cleaning, e-commerce, employment agencies, fast food, formal wear rental, gas stations, greeting cards, grocery sales, hair care, hardware, home remodeling, insurance, lawn care, lumber and building, maid services, music sales, oil lubrication, optical care, photo processing, photocopying, real estate, restaurants, telephone networks, tax preparation, tire sales, security systems, swimming pool sales, travel agencies, and weight loss centers.

While the list of industries in which franchising takes place is impressive—and with franchising spread over 80 industries, the breadth of this organizational form is quite large—franchising is far from a universally applicable way of doing business. Franchising does not occur in literally hundreds of industries. Moreover, franchising is

1

highly concentrated in just a few industries. One study from the International Franchise Association reports that 18 percent of all franchise systems are found in fast food and 11 percent are found in general retail.[1] Other data sources provide similar results. Table 1.1 summarizes the percentages of franchisors for the most popular industries for franchising as reported in the *Sourcebook of Franchise Opportunities*.

TABLE 1.1   The Top Ten Industries for Franchising in Percentage of Franchisors

Industry	Percent of Franchisors	Percent of Franchised Units
Fast food	15.2	26.8
Restaurants	7.0	3.8
Automotive products	6.2	5.5
Maintenance and cleaning	5.4	8.2
Building and remodeling	4.9	1.5
Specialty retail	3.8	1.5
Specialty food	3.8	2.0
Health and fitness	3.3	3.5
Child development	3.2	0.7
Lodging	3.1	5.9

Source: Adapted from data contained in R. Bond's *Bond's Franchise Guide, 15th Annual Edition* (Oakland, CA: Sourcebook Publications, 2004). 14–15.

Other evidence shows that franchisors perform much better in certain industries than in others. Franchisors now account for the majority of sales in tax preparation, printing and copying, and specialty food retailing, and close to half of all sales in restaurants and lodging.[2] This suggests that these industries are particularly good ones for franchising. Several research studies also demonstrate the favorability of certain industries for franchising. In a report to the Office of Advocacy of the U.S. Small Business Administration, I showed that new food franchisors have a higher 12-year survival rate than retail or service franchisors.[3] Similarly, FRANDATA Corporation, a franchise consulting firm, examined franchisor bankruptcies from 1983 to 1993 and found that 17.4 percent of lodging franchisors had gone bankrupt, as compared to only 12.5 percent of restaurants and less than 5 percent of business franchisors.[4]

The somewhat limited range of industries in which franchising operates, combined with the concentration of franchising in a handful of industries and the evidence of better franchisor performance in some industries than in others, suggests that an important issue for you, as a potential franchisor, is to determine whether franchising is appropriate for the industry in which you operate. This chapter identifies nine characteristics that make franchising appropriate for an industry:

- Production and distribution occur in limited geographic markets.
- Physical locations are helpful to serving customers.
- Local market knowledge is important to performance.
- Local management discretion is beneficial.
- Brand name reputation is a valuable competitive advantage.
- The level of standardization and codification of the process of creating and delivering the product or service is high.
- The operation is labor intensive.
- Outlets are not terribly costly or risky to establish.
- The effort of outlet operators is hard to measure relative to their performance.

Before discussing the characteristics that make some industries more appropriate for franchising than others, however, the chapter first defines franchising and gives a short history of how it evolved and became a part of the business landscape.

What Is Franchising?

In casual terms, a franchise is a particular legal form of organization in which the development of a business concept and its execution are undertaken by two different legal entities. Of course, franchising is a legal arrangement, and the Federal Trade Commission, the U.S. government agency responsible for regulating franchising, provides a legal definition of this arrangement. According to the Federal Trade Commission Rule 436.2, paragraph 6160:

> "The term 'franchise' means any commercial relationship... whereby a person offers, sells or distributes to any person...goods, commodities, or services which are: (1) identified by a trademark service mark, trade name, advertising or other commercial symbol...or (2) directly or indirectly required or advised to meet the quality standards prescribed by another person where the franchisee operates under a name using the trademark, service mark, trade name, advertising, or other commercial symbol."

The broad category of franchising is made up of two different business models: product franchising and business format franchising. Product franchising is an arrangement in which one party, a franchisor, develops a trade name and licenses it to another party, a franchisee. The product franchisee contracts for the use of the name to deliver products or services to end customers for a certain time period at a certain location. Examples of companies that engage in product franchising are Coca-Cola®, Goodyear Tires, and John Deere.

Business format franchising is an arrangement in which one party, a franchisor, develops a brand name and an operating system for a business, and licenses them to another party, a franchisee. The franchisee contracts for the use of the name and the operating system to deliver products or services to end customers for a certain time period and at a certain location. Examples of companies that engage in business format franchising are General Nutrition Centers®, Jiffy Lube®, MAACO®, McDonald's, Subway®, Uniglobe® Travel, and Wendy's®.

The major difference between product franchising and business format franchising is that product franchisors do not offer an operating system to franchisees, and business format franchisors do. Because product franchisors do not license an operating system to franchisees, they do not seek uniformity in the operations of their franchisees. Another difference between the two types of franchisors is that product franchisors tend to seek compensation from sales of products to franchisees who resell them to retail customers, whereas business format franchisors tend to make money from royalties on gross sales to retail customers.[5] However, this latter difference tends to be blurred because a significant minority of business format franchisors makes at least some profits from the sale of inputs to their franchisees.

As will be explained in more detail later, franchising is most common in industries in which companies need to operate a large number of outlets across a wide variety of geographic locations. This means that franchising is very common among the chain organizations that dot the business landscape. But not all chains need to be franchised. As was mentioned in the "Introduction," Starbucks manages an enormous retail coffee chain without franchising a single outlet.

A Very Brief History of Franchising

Most business historians date the beginning of franchising as a concept to the Middle Ages, when feudal lords initiated the practice of selling to others the rights to collect taxes and operate markets on their behalf. However, this makes the earliest examples of franchising a political activity rather than a business activity. The first examples of franchising as a way of doing business are found in mid-nineteenth century Germany, where brewers set up contracts with tavern owners to sell their beer exclusively in the taverns.

In the United States, the earliest example of the use of franchising was not found in breweries and taverns. Instead, it occurred in the sale of products to housewives located on the American prairie. In 1851, Isaac Singer became the first American product name franchisor when he began to sell to traveling independent salesmen the rights to sell his sewing machines to end users.

Although the Singer® Sewing Machine Company was the earliest American product name franchisor, it was relatively quickly outpaced by an even more important product name franchisor: Coca-Cola. In the early 1890s, Coca-Cola chose to franchise the rights to bottle its carbonated beverage to a large number of independent businessmen who received exclusive territories in which to distribute the product in return for paying for and assuming the risk of, distributing the product.[6]

Certainly, Coca-Cola was an important early product name franchisor, but it might not have been the most important one to begin operations at the turn of the 20th century. That distinction might be reserved for the pioneers in the American automobile industry, which began to franchise at that time. Both Ford and General Motors began to franchise dealerships to independent business people to sell cars under their brand names to end users because the companies did not have sufficient funds to create the needed retail outlets when they first began operations.

Another important innovation in franchising was the development of conversion franchising. Conversion franchising is the process of turning independent businesses into franchisees under the umbrella of the franchisor's brand name. The major oil companies were the pioneers in this activity when they began to offer independent repair stations the right to use their trademarks in the 1920s.[7]

We can also date several other pioneers in franchising in retail and service businesses to the 1920s and 1930s. Perhaps the earliest retail franchisor is Ben Franklin stores, which started in 1920 and began to franchise around that time. The earliest fast food franchise was A&W® Root Beer, established in 1924, with Howard Johnson® being the first to franchise restaurants in 1935. An early pioneer in service franchising was Arthur Murray® Dance Studios, which got its start in 1938.

Franchising really took off as a form of business in the 1950s and 1960s, when many of the current large franchise chains, businesses such as Tastee-Freez®, KFC®, McDonald's, and Burger King®, were established. The acceleration of franchising in the 1950s and 1960s can be attributed largely to two factors: the rise of television advertising and the establishment of the national highway system. The former made national advertising a viable way to build a brand name. As a result, for the first time, it became possible to have a national chain whose competitive advantage was based on a recognizable name. The latter made travel to unfamiliar locations more common and created the need to have national brand names as a way to demonstrate quality to customers in these locations.

Perhaps because of the growth of franchising in the 1960s, that decade witnessed the formation of a flurry of fly-by-night franchise operations that established their systems, sold them to franchisees, took the franchisees' money, and quickly shut down. The loss of many people's investment in these franchises led to the beginning of franchise regulation in the 1970s. The Federal Trade Commission (FTC) initiated its first franchise fraud investigations in 1975. In that same year, the North American Securities Administration drew up draft guidelines for Uniform Franchise Offering Circulars (UFOCs), which have become the standard form for disclosing franchise opportunities to franchisees. This growing federal effort in the 1970s also culminated in the establishment of disclosure requirements and business rules for selling franchises by the FTC in 1979 and the start of the regulated era of franchising. As a result of this effort, franchising is now a regulated form of business, making an understanding of the legal environment in which it operates important to you as a franchisor.

Local Production in Limited Geographic Markets

Franchising makes more sense in industries in which providing customers with a product or service requires small-scale production and distribution in a wide variety of different geographic locations. This is why franchising does not occur in most manufacturing industries. Most manufactured products can be created in large volume in a central location and shipped around the world from that location.[8] In most manufacturing industries, the right incentives and controls needed to deliver a large volume of a standardized product to customers can be put in place without franchising.

However, in other industries, such as fast food, the product and services provided to customers cannot all be delivered from a centralized spot; they must be provided from a variety of different locations. Providing the right incentives and controls to deliver a large volume of a standardized product to customers in these industries can be enhanced by franchising. Therefore, franchising is much more likely to occur in retail and service businesses than in manufacturing businesses.

Moreover, within the set of all retail and service businesses, franchising tends to work best where some aspect of the operation, such as building the brand name or sourcing supply, is subject to economies of scale, but production and distribution need to take place on a small scale in a variety of different locations. As a result, some aspects of the operation benefit from centralization, while local outlets provide a way to deliver the product or service to end customers. The restaurant industry provides a good example. The brand names that attract customers are subject to significant economies of scale. However, the production and distribution of meals takes place on a small scale in a variety of locations because people won't travel very far for a restaurant meal.

One of the effects of being in an industry in which production and distribution occur on a small scale in a variety of locations is that businesses face severe limits on the growth of sales at individual locations. You might be able to grow your semiconductor plant dramatically and ship your products around the world, but you are not going to be able to grow sales at your restaurant very much without adding another location. Your product cannot be shipped to another location, and people will travel only so far to get your product, limiting the number of customers in your geographic market.

To grow sales in industries in which the potential for sales growth at existing locations is quite limited, entrepreneurs and managers need to increase the number of locations that their businesses operate. Franchising is a very effective strategy in businesses where sales growth tends not to come from expansion of sales at existing units, but from unit growth.[9] For reasons that will be discussed in greater detail in the next chapter, franchising makes it possible to add outlets with less management supervision than is the case without franchising.

Stop! Don't Do It!

1. Don't franchise unless your industry requires some activities subject to scale economies and others that require local activities in a limited geographic area.
2. Don't franchise in an industry in which sales growth comes easily from expansion of operations at existing locations.

Physical Locations Are Helpful

Franchising is more effective in industries such as computer stores, in which the product or service is provided to the end customer at a set location, than in industries such as carpet cleaning services, in which the product or service is provided at the customer's premises.

While franchising can, and does, occur in service industries without set locations for production and distribution, it is harder to minimize conflict between franchisees in such industries. Franchisees are independent businesses, so they have incentives to compete with each other to serve the same customers, a situation that is not present when the same party owns the different locations.

Franchisors cannot prevent their franchisees from competing with each other. While antitrust laws allow franchisors to refrain from putting an additional franchised or company-owned outlet in a particular geographic area, these laws preclude franchisors from limiting efforts of franchisees to serve customers in one location from another location.[10]

In businesses in which it is difficult to serve customers from a distant physical location, franchisors can effectively minimize between-franchisee competition by limiting the number of locations in a geographic area. Take, for example, the situation with McDonald's outlets. Because you need to go to the neighborhood McDonald's to get your burger fix, there is little between-franchisee competition for your burger business. Another McDonald's franchisee on the other side of town is unlikely to be able to sell you the burger that you are planning to have for lunch.

However, when the franchisee's physical location doesn't matter for the production and delivery of a product or service to the end customer (usually because the production and delivery occur at the customer's premises), franchisees end up competing with each other for the same customers. For instance, online travel agency franchises face the problem of franchisees from one city selling cruise and Disney vacations to customers in another city. That problem makes franchising relatively ineffective in the online travel agency business. In short, in industries that do not require a fixed location to produce and deliver a product or service to the end customer, having a vertical organization in which managers can tell subordinates not to compete with each other for customers is often necessary to avoid between-location competition. Franchising is not as effective in these industries as it is in industries in which fixed locations are needed for production and distribution.

Industries Involving Local Knowledge

Franchising tends to be more effective in industries in which local market knowledge is more important to business success than in other industries. Because the franchisee comes from the local market, he or she can provide information about needed adaptations to the market more cheaply than a centralized company can search for it. Moreover, as owners, franchisees profit from adapting products or services to meet the needs of local markets and thus have stronger incentives to do so than hired employees.

A good example of the incentives that franchisees have to adapt their products to local market needs in industries in which local market knowledge is important is the story of the Cincinnati franchisee who developed the McDonald's Filet-O-Fish® sandwich. Faced with a significant drop-off in Friday sales during Lent at his restaurant in a predominantly Catholic neighborhood, Cincinnati franchisee Lou Groen developed the fish sandwich to recapture customers who were going to other restaurants in search of meatless meals.[11] Of course, this sandwich turned out to be a big success and was later transplanted worldwide by the McDonald's Corporation.

Industries Demanding Local Discretion

Franchising tends to be more effective in industries such as equipment rental or formalwear rentals, in which fixed prices and a standardized approach work poorly, and managerial discretion to negotiate with customers is very important to making sales.[12] To make sales in these types of industries, the person negotiating with customers needs to be given a strong incentive to take actions and make decisions that will result in sales. Franchising is effective in this situation because it replaces, as the party negotiating with the customer, a hired employee whose compensation is not affected by the number of sales made or the price at which they occur, with an entrepreneur who will benefit from making only profitable sales.

Stop! Don't Do It!

1. Don't franchise unless customers in your industry are served from fixed locations; otherwise your franchisees will end up fighting with each other over customers and you won't be able to stop them.

2. Don't own outlets in industries in which you need to give outlet operators an incentive to adapt products to local markets; franchising provides them with an incentive to do that.

3. Don't own outlets in industries in which outlet operators need discretion to negotiate with customers; salaried managers won't have the right incentive to do that well.

Standardized, Codified, and Easily Learned

Although franchising works better in industries in which local discretion in the process of selling to customers is more important, that does not mean it works well in industries in which products or services need to be customized. Rather, franchising works best in industries with standardized products and services. Standardization makes it easier to determine the right policies and procedures for monitoring the actions of independent businesspeople (the franchisees), who are serving customers under the system's brand name and using its operating procedures. By standardizing operations, it is easy to set down in a contract exactly what the franchisee is expected to do. If he or she deviates from this standardized approach, the franchisor can terminate the franchisee's right to operate the outlet and sell it to someone who will follow the rules. Without standardized operations, it is hard to know whether the deviation of the franchisee is inappropriate; this makes it difficult to write contracts specifying franchisee actions and even harder to enforce those contracts after they are written.

This preference for franchising in industries in which products or services are standardized is why we tend to see franchising in services such as tax preparation but not in medical care. The process for filling out tax forms can be standardized, facilitating contracting and monitoring. The process for doing heart surgery cannot be standardized, and the failure to customize when necessary can have very severe adverse results. As a result, contracting how to do heart surgery is difficult, and monitoring the behavior of heart surgeons is too difficult to make franchising of much value.

Franchising also works better in industries in which the operation of the business can be codified. Codification is the process of writing something down. Codifying a business operation means writing down the routines and procedures underlying the operation, from the ordering of supplies to the serving of customers, to the repairing of machinery. For example, Krispy Kreme gives its franchisees specific donut recipes, as well as procedures for how and when to make the donuts. Franchising is more effective in industries in which the routines and procedures can be codified because the mode of business depends on the ability to write contracts to govern the actions and obligations of franchisors and franchisees. To control your franchisees' behavior and ensure that your standards are being upheld, you need to write down those standards in the contract you sign with them. Moreover, when you franchise, one of the things that you lease to your franchisees is an operating manual, or written set of procedures for running the business.

Franchising also requires an industry in which an average person can learn the operation of the business with only the training that you, the franchisor, provide in a few days or weeks. For instance, Subway

Restaurants, the world's largest franchisor, provides only two weeks of training to its franchisees before sending them off to run their own businesses. The need for short training periods is one thing that makes franchising more effective in industries such as fast food and tutoring than in industries that require detailed knowledge or long-term training, such as dentistry or higher education.

Moreover, to have a big enough pool of potential franchisees to sell franchises to, you need a business that you can train the majority of the population to run, not just a small group of people with specialized skills. For example, franchising tends to work most effectively in industries in which a general high school education is all that people need to work in the industry, as is the case with ice cream shops. Industries that require a great deal of training and skill development, such as plumbing and electrical contracting, are less amenable to franchising. Because of the time it takes to learn to be a plumber or an electrician, and the relatively small number of people with the skills to perform these trades, these industries are the not the best ones for franchising.

Brand Names: An Important Competitive Advantage

Franchising is most effective in industries in which brand name development is important. This is the case in fragmented industries, such as restaurants. In fragmented industries, the development of a brand name is often an important competitive advantage to firms that lack other ways to differentiate themselves from their competition.[13]

Franchising is valuable in industries in which brand names are important because it increases the scale of operations of a business very quickly—much more quickly, in fact, than through company ownership of outlets. Because building a brand name relies heavily on advertising, which is influenced by scale economies, franchising provides a mechanism for lowering the costs of building a company's brand name.

In addition, brand names provide a way for customers who have little information about providers in particular markets—such as tourists looking for a meal—to ensure quality. By providing a common brand umbrella for businesses operating in unfamiliar areas, you can ensure that your customers will know what they will experience before they pay for that experience. That, of course, makes them more willing to commit to purchasing your product or service. In short, franchising provides a much greater advantage to firms in industries in which brand names are an important competitive advantage. This leads franchising to be concentrated in these industries.

Labor-Intensive Industries

Franchising is a very useful method of business in labor-intensive industries and is less valuable in capital-intensive ones. For instance, a large number of maid services (with their low equipment-to-staff ratios) are franchised, but very few health clubs (with their high equipment-to-staff ratios) are franchised. As you have probably noticed, people often shirk, failing to work as hard or as diligently as they can. Machines, on the other hand, do not shirk. Shirking is often combated by giving people incentives to perform, such as compensating them from the profits of their effort. Perform, and they earn a lot; shirk, and they do not. Of course, giving people incentives to perform is what franchising does. It makes the operator of an outlet a residual claimant on the profits of the outlet rather than a wage employee. So franchising motivates the operators of outlets not to shirk. Because people shirk but machines do not, the incentives provided by franchising are more important in labor-intensive industries than in capital-intensive ones. Therefore, the franchising mode of doing business is most appropriate in labor-intensive industries.

Moreover, franchising gives outlet operators an incentive to monitor costs more closely than hired managers. Because franchisees keep the profits from their operations after all costs are subtracted from revenues, they have a very strong incentive to keep costs down. This means that franchisees often watch their employees more carefully than managers do. They also tend to hire family members at less than market wages, as a way to cut costs. The more labor intensive the industry is, the greater is the effect of efforts to hire inexpensive labor or monitor costs as a way to improve the profitability of a business. This is one reason why we tend to see franchising in labor-intensive industries such as household maintenance and cleaning, but not in capital-intensive ones such as construction.

Stop! Don't Do It!

1. Don't fight the odds; franchising works best in industries in which knowledge is standardized, codified, and easy to learn.

2. Don't own outlets in industries in which brand names are a key competitive advantage; you will benefit from franchising in these industries.

3. Don't franchise in a capital-intensive industry; you will achieve few benefits from it.

4. Don't ignore the value of franchising as a way to keep costs down.

Cost and Risk

Franchising works best in industries in which outlets are neither very expensive nor very risky for people to operate. In fact, research has shown that, in industries in which outlets are larger in terms of employment, sales, or physical space, firms tend to franchise less than firms in industries in which outlets are smaller.[14] For instance, in industries in which the cost of establishing a single outlet is in the tens or hundreds of millions of dollars (industries such as retail appliance sales), franchising is relatively uncommon. Not only is there a small pool of potential franchisees with enough money to purchase franchises in such industries, but the very high investment also leads franchisees to underinvest in the development of the outlet. This problem of underinvestment is discussed in more detail in Chapter 3, "The Disadvantages of Franchising," but let's suffice it to say here that individual franchisees who make large investments are undiversified and, thus, are more risk averse than corporations that have raised money for all of their outlets simultaneously. This lack of diversification leads them to see a given investment as more risky than diversified investors see it and keeps them from making the investments that diversified investors would make.

For similar reasons, franchising works poorly in industries with a high level of risk resulting from factors outside the franchisee's control, such as variation in the general economic environment. For example, franchising doesn't work very well in the mortgage brokerage business because performance at refinancing homes depends a lot on interest rates on mortgages, which franchisees cannot control.

Franchising works poorly in these types of industries because high levels of environmental risk make franchises difficult to sell. A franchisee makes an investment in buying an outlet to earn financial return on that investment. The performance of the franchisee's investment is affected by both the person's own performance and the effect of factors beyond the franchisee's control, such as the condition of the economy. Diversification is the main mechanism that investors have to deal with the effect of factors beyond their control. Because the investments of franchisees are undiversified—they generally buy into only one franchise system at a time—they tend to be unwilling or unable to bear the risk of things beyond their own control. As a result, they tend not to buy franchises in industries in which this type of risk is very high. Diversified corporations are more able to bear this type of risk, so we see company-owned operations in industries with high levels of general economic risk.

Measuring Performance

Companies generally have two ways of evaluating people: measuring the level of their effort and measuring the level of their performance. Franchising works best in industries such as retail, in which measuring the level of people's performance can be done easily and effectively, but measuring their effort is more difficult. For example, franchising works well in fast food because sales, which are easy to measure, tend to increase when people work harder at advertising and promoting a business and when they maintain efficiency and cleanliness in outlets, even though things such as the effort that they expended to clean the outlets or promote the products are hard to measure.

On the other hand, in industries in which the level of people's performance is hard to measure, franchising is a less valuable form of business.[15] When measures of performance are not instantaneous or are unclear, company ownership of outlets is better because the profit motive is not very effective at motivating people to work hard. For example, suppose that developing a new production process would benefit a business, but its effect on increasing sales or cutting costs is unclear. Franchising would not be a very good mode of business in this example because the incentives of franchisees to develop the new production process would be low. Their compensation from franchising would not be affected much by the thing the franchisor was trying to motivate them to do: develop a new production process.

Measures of performance are more effective with businesses that operate in more markets. As a result, franchising works better in industries that are found in a wider range of geographic locations than in ones found in a narrow range of places. For example, franchising works extremely well in the restaurant and fast food industries because these businesses can be located anywhere—inside malls, strip centers, stadiums, universities, hospitals, and so on. The more geographically dispersed industries are, the greater the variation in business environments firms in those industries face. This variation in the external environment helps the entity measuring performance—in this case, the franchisor—to separate the effect of the environment from the effect of the performer, allowing more accurate measurement of the effect of the performer. Thus, in industries in which outlets are found in all locations in the world—say, ice cream parlors—the value of franchising is greater than in ones found only in a few places—say, apartment rental services.

Stop! Don't Do It!

1. Don't franchise in a capital intensive industry; you will achieve few benefits from it.
2. Don't ignore the value of franchising as a way to keep costs down.
3. Don't franchise in industries in which measures of effort are better indicators than measures of output.
4. Don't franchise in industries that operate in only narrow geographic environments; the narrowness will hinder the measurement of performance.

Questions to Ask Yourself

1. Is my industry appropriate for franchising?
2. Are the production and distribution processes in my industry favorable to franchising?
3. Are the operations of businesses in my industry easily standardized, codified, and learned by others?
4. Is my industry labor or capital intensive?
5. Are brand names an important competitive advantage in my industry?
6. Are outlets in my industry too expensive and too risky to operate for me to franchise?
7. Can performance of outlet operators be measured effectively in my industry?

Summary

This chapter explained that a franchise is a particular legal form of organization in which the development of a business concept and its execution are undertaken by two different legal entities: the franchisor, which provides the trade name, and the franchisee, which delivers the product or service under that name. The broad category of franchising is composed of product franchising, which does not involve the provision of an operating system to franchisees along with trade name, and business format franchising, which does.

Most business historians date the beginning of franchising to the Middle Ages, when feudal lords initiated the practice of selling to others the rights to collect taxes and operate markets on their behalf. In the United States, the earliest business use of franchising dates to 1851, when Isaac Singer began his sewing machine company. However, franchising did not enter widespread use in the United States until the turn of the twentieth century, when auto manufacturers began to use this business model with their dealerships. The most dramatic growth in franchising occurred in the 1950s and 1960s, when many of the current large franchise chains were established.

The first rule of successful franchising is to make sure that your industry is appropriate for franchising. Some industries are simply better than others for the creation of franchise chains. Almost 56 percent of franchisors are concentrated in the top ten industries for franchising: fast food, restaurants, automotive products, maintenance and cleaning, building and remodeling, specialty retail, specialty food, health and fitness, child development, and lodging. In some industries, such as tax preparation, printing and copying, and specialty food retailing, franchisors now account for the majority of all firms.

Researchers have identified nine industry characteristics that make franchising appropriate: Production and distribution occur in limited geographic markets; physical locations are helpful to serving customers; local market knowledge is important to performance;

local management discretion is beneficial; brand name reputation is a valuable competitive advantage; the level of standardization and codification of the process of creating and delivering the product or service is high; the operation is labor intensive, outlets are not terribly costly or risky to establish; and the effort of outlet operators is hard to measure relative to their performance.

Franchising makes more sense in industries in which providing customers with a product or service requires small-scale production and distribution in a wide variety of different geographic locations, particularly where some aspect of production—such as creating the brand name or sourcing supply—is subject to economies of scale. Franchising also works better in industries in which customers are served from a fixed geographic location than when they are not.

Because local production is a necessary component for franchising to work well in an industry, franchising tends to be more useful in industries in which local knowledge and local managerial discretion are important to business success. At the same time, however, franchising requires an industry in which the creation and delivery of products or services can be standardized, codified, and easily learned.

Franchising is more effective in industries in which brand name development is important than in ones in which brand names are not a source of competitive advantage. It also works better in labor-intensive industries than in capital-intensive ones. Franchising does not work well in industries in which outlets are costly or risky to operate. Finally, franchising works better in industries in which performance can be measured more easily than effort, than it does in industries in which the inverse is true.

Now that you understand rule number one of franchising, making sure that your industry is appropriate for franchising, we now turn to rule number two, understanding the advantages of franchising. This is the subject of the next chapter.

2

THE ADVANTAGES
OF FRANCHISING

As with many modes of doing business, franchising has its advantages and its disadvantages. Successful entrepreneurs and managers understand the advantages of franchising and compare them to the disadvantages to determine whether to adopt franchising in their firms. This chapter explores the pros of franchising, while Chapter 3, "The Disadvantages of Franchising," discusses the cons of this organizational arrangement.

For franchising to be advantageous, two conditions must be met. First, a chain of outlets must be superior to independent businesses seeking to serve customer needs (perhaps because standardized procedures and the system brand name give the chain an advantage). Second, the chain must be better organized through ownership by independent operators rather than by employed managers. The second of these conditions is the most important and is the focus of this chapter.

Although franchising is useful to firms in a variety of ways, in general, it provides three categories of advantages to firms:

1. It provides a better mechanism for selecting and offering incentives to outlet operators than salaried employment.

2. It offers an efficient mechanism for obtaining human and financial resources for rapid firm growth.

3. It offers a lucrative economic model, generating financial returns at relatively low risk.

Selecting and Providing Incentives to Outlet Operators

Franchising is a useful tool for generating high performance. The benefits of franchising operate through two mechanisms: Franchising encourages self-selection of qualified people to positions managing outlets, making it easier for entrepreneurs and managers of chains to find highly qualified operators. It also offers a strong incentive to encourage the performance of those outlet operators: the profit motive.

Effective Selection

Franchising provides an important human resource advantage to firms: It reduces the difficulty and cost of selecting highly competent outlet operators. When a firm looks to hire employees, it faces a problem that economists call *adverse selection*. Adverse selection is the tendency of people who have lesser abilities to put themselves forward as candidates for jobs more often than the overall population of job seekers. As a result, the entrepreneurs and managers who select employees have to incur significant costs to identify the right candidates: those with the skills and abilities to do the job.

Take, for example, a company that provides printing and copying services. Because the managers of a printing and copying shop are generally paid a flat salary, those people with lesser abilities at managing one of these shops have a greater incentive to apply for the job as a shop manager than those people with greater print and copy shop management ability. Why? The job of shop manager is paid a higher salary than the people with lesser ability can get otherwise; however, this is not true for the people of greater ability. So the financial returns of getting the job are greater for the people of lesser ability than the people of greater ability.

Moreover, if the people of lesser ability get a job for which they are unqualified, any costs of that error are borne by the employer, not by them. This means that for an entrepreneur or manager to identify qualified candidates from a pool that includes unqualified ones, he or she has to expend time and effort screening potential employees by using applications, conducting interviews, and verifying references. Moreover, because these screens are only partially effective, the company could end up hiring a person who is unqualified for the job.

Franchising goes a long way toward mitigating this selection problem. When a person becomes a franchisee of a print and copy shop (or any other business), he or she makes a financial investment in purchasing the franchise and then makes a profit on the operation of the outlet. Those people who do not have print and copy shop management capabilities will not make as much of a profit from this investment and could even lose the capital that they invested in the outlet. On the other hand, people who have the print and copy shop management capabilities will be likely to earn high returns on their investments. As a result, those people who try to buy franchises tend to be the most qualified candidates, and those who are the least qualified candidates shy away from making an investment. This makes franchising a very inexpensive and effective way to select good outlet operators.[1]

Better Incentives

Companies often face a problem that economists call *shirking*, a situation in which employees do not put forth the amount of effort that they are capable of providing. The major reason that employees shirk is that they will receive the same compensation whether or not they work hard.

The fact that shirking occurs from a lack of compensation for performance makes franchising an excellent tool for minimizing the problem. By replacing a salaried manager with an entrepreneur whose compensation comes from profits of operating an outlet, you can minimize the incentive of the operators of your outlets to shirk. Because franchisees own their outlets, they have an incentive to work harder than the employees at company-owned outlets. The cost of their shirking is borne by them. If your franchisee shirks instead of working hard, his or her profits will fall, cutting his or her compensation.[2]

Franchising also increases sales by providing an incentive for outlet operators to innovate in ways that meet the needs of the local market. Because they spend their days interacting with customers in the local market, outlet operators often have information that is valuable to a firm's effort to modify its product or service to meet the needs of the customers in that market. Franchising provides the outlet operator with an incentive to make use of this information. The ownership that franchisees have in their outlets makes them sensitive to information that would help them increase sales in their local market. By finding a valuable innovation and implementing it in his or her outlet, the franchisee has the opportunity to earn greater profits. In contrast, a straight-salaried employee gets nothing for innovating and, therefore, has no incentive to pay attention to how to adapt products or services to local market conditions.[3]

Because franchising has a strong effect on reducing shirking, it provides a very effective incentive for increasing sales at retail outlets.

One study by Timothy Bates of Wayne State University showed that the mean level of sales at franchised restaurants was 82 percent higher than the mean level of sales at nonfranchised restaurants.[4] So one of the real benefit of franchising is encouraging the people operating retail outlets to work harder and increase sales.

Although the biggest incentive effect of franchising lies in its effect on increasing sales either by encouraging hard work or by motivating innovation at the local level, it has several other benefits that enhance performance. The profit motive gives franchisees an incentive to set a high pace for work among their employees. Because franchisees capture the profits from the performance of their outlets, they have a strong incentive to increase the pace of work if that pace is important to enhancing the performance of the business. In a business such as auto repair, in which the franchisee has made a sizable investment in equipment, the effort to set a faster work pace enhances the profitability of the business because it makes the investment in the business's capital much more efficient.

Moreover, franchisees have an incentive to keep costs down and keep labor costs below what they are in company-owned outlets. Because profits are the residual when costs are subtracted from revenues, franchisees are keen to do anything that lowers their costs. This often means making sure that they do not overpay for raw materials or for labor. Research supports this proposition. One study of fast food franchises showed that shift managers earned 9 percent more in the company-owned outlets of the same chains than they did in the franchised ones.[5] The tendency of local general managers of company-owned outlets to pay their shift managers more than franchisees pay for the same work indicates that franchisees are more careful with money, probably because any savings that are accrued from keeping shift manager compensation in line goes into the pockets of franchisees, but has no effect on the compensation of local general managers of company-owned outlets.

Why, you might ask, can't companies use other mechanisms, such as bonuses or stock options, instead of franchising as a way to provide incentives to employees not to shirk? The answer is that these incentives are beneficial, but they don't work as well as franchising to motivate outlet operators to make decisions that enhance performance. When an employee doesn't buy the equity in a business that he or she receives, as is the case with stock options, he or she isn't likely to care about downside risk. As a result, compensating employees with stock options encourages outlet operators to take risky actions with high upside potential but also high downside potential. After all, in those situations, the employee will get the benefit of the upside without bearing the cost of the downside. With franchising, these excessively risky actions are discouraged because the franchisee bears the costs of the downside as well as the benefits of the upside.

Bonuses generate a different kind of problem from stock options that limits their effectiveness as an incentive. Bonuses provide an incentive by giving employees extra compensation for performance improvements that they make. However, they do not give employees a claim on the future profit of an outlet when it is sold. Therefore, bonuses bias employees toward performance improvements that occur in the present rather than improvements in the future value of the outlet.[6] This makes salaried managers more shortsighted about actions that improve performance than is the case with franchisees, who would receive some portion of future earnings from the expected sale of a franchised outlet.

Another one of the real benefits of franchising is that the information that outlet operators collect about local market conditions and their effect on the business—things such as the hours an outlet should be open, the wages that should be paid to employees, and the best inputs and sources of supply to use—flows to the headquarters of the company much more easily and effectively if the company engages in franchising than if its outlet operators are employees. Why? The answer has to do with the hierarchies that companies have to establish to manage their operations. Because managers face limits on their spans of control (they can supervise only so many people before they run out of time), firms need to create a hierarchy of employees to supervise operations when they grow. However, the use of hierarchies to manage larger operations leads information to get distorted as it travels up the organization. Each time a piece of information travels up through the organization, the people passing on the information filter that information through their own perceptions and frame it to support their own goals and agendas, leading that information to become distorted. (Remember the old children's game of telephone?)

Franchising mitigates this problem. Because franchisees are independent businesspeople who have established contracts to conduct business as the franchisor's partner, they have direct access to the top management of chain organization. This allows them to communicate directly with the senior team of a chain organization, something that is rarely possible for the employee-managers of outlets, even in the same organization. Because the views of franchisees are communicated directly to the senior management of a chain, the information that they provide is less distorted by the middle management of the organization than is the information provided by employee-managers.

In addition, managers at chain organizations achieve much greater spans of control over franchisees than they can over employee-managers—as much as six times as large. This allows chains to have far fewer levels of hierarchy through which information must travel when they use franchising. The greater spans of control result from the fact that franchising gives such strong incentives to franchisees and also the fact that franchisees operate independent businesses, leading them to require much less interaction and assistance from headquarters than employee-managers. As a result, when franchising is used, there are fewer layers of organization to distort information than when franchising is not employed.

Finally, franchising reduces the level of gaming of information by outlet operators. Because franchisees are independent entrepreneurs, they are more likely than salaried employees to tell the top management of the chain what they really believe to be true than they are to simply agree with the senior managers as a way of playing the organization politics necessary to get a raise or promotion. As a result, the information transmitted to the top managers of a chain organization tends to be much more accurate when businesses are franchised than when they are not.

Stop! Don't Do It!

1. Don't use company-owned outlets when it is difficult and costly to select people to operate your business; franchising provides an inexpensive and effective solution to selection problems.

2. Don't use company-owned outlets when your employees have an incentive to shirk or when you want local market adaptation; franchising is very effective in these situations.

Obtaining Resources for Rapid Growth

Franchising is an important mechanism for obtaining the financial and human resources that firms need for rapid growth. However, before we get into a discussion of how franchising facilitates rapid growth, it is important to first explain why growing quickly is important for franchisors. In industries in which brand names are an important form of the competitive advantage, firms need to grow quickly. Advertising is subject to significant economies of scale, but the average new firm in industries in which advertising is important is much smaller than the average existing firm. Therefore, rapid growth is important for firms to reach minimum efficient scale for advertising to promote their brand names in a cost-effective manner.

Growth is also important for firms because it makes them more likely to reach a size at which they can get the advantages of bulk purchasing of inputs. Larger companies often have greater bargaining power with resource providers and so can purchase inputs at a lower cost than their smaller counterparts. This is especially true for commodities for which volume purchasing greatly reduces cost. For instance, Jiffy Lube has much lower cost for the motor oil it buys than independent service stations because it purchases motor oil in many times larger quantities than those stations.[7]

Growth also helps businesses when they have a high fixed cost of development relative to the marginal cost of additional applications. For example, the cost of developing recipes for a new restaurant is relatively high compared to the marginal cost of exploiting the recipes in additional locations. As a result, system growth reduces the average cost of serving meals, making the business more profitable as it grows.

A final reason for rapid growth is to gain access to desirable locations before they are acquired by the competition. In many businesses, good locations are very important but are in short supply. For instance, a particular intersection in a particular town might be an ideal spot for a restaurant, or traffic patterns might make a particular mall crucial for retail sales in a city. By growing quickly, firms can lock down these desirable locations before they are snatched up by other firms.

Now that you understand why growth is important for many businesses, we need to turn attention to how franchising helps firms to grow rapidly. Research shows that franchising not only helps firms to grow the size of their businesses more rapidly than if they own their own outlets, but it also allows companies to grow at rates that are, in fact, astounding. For example, by franchising exclusively, Subway Sandwich Shops grew from 150 to 19,239 outlets between 1980 and 2004, a rate of growth of 12,260 percent![8]

Capital Acquisition

Franchising allows companies to grow rapidly by allowing them to add outlets at a much lower capital expense than would otherwise be the case. Franchisees provide franchisors with up-front fees every time the franchisor adds an additional (franchised) outlet. More important, franchisees pay for many of the costs of adding outlets, including such things as the cost of setting up the location and obtaining initial inventory.

The capital savings that firms reap by passing the costs of establishing outlets on to their franchisees can be very large. For example, in the restaurant industry, in which each outlet might cost $500,000 to establish, the ability to franchise might make it possible to create a chain of 100 outlets, requiring $50,000,000 in capital, all paid for with franchisee money.

Moreover, franchising allows the franchisor to avoid raising a large amount of debt to create the chain of outlets. Minimizing the acquisition of debt, in turn, reduces the degree to which a company is leveraged. This is valuable to companies because companies need to make fixed-interest payments on a regular basis. The variability of sales in many industries means that the ability to avoid fixed-interest payments is of strategic value to firms.

Franchising also overcomes many of the constraints that young firms face in raising capital for expansion. Often young firms cannot obtain adequate capital from financial markets because investors will not bear the risks inherent in backing these companies. Sometimes this problem occurs when firms enter industries that are new to chain operations, leading investors to perceive the new firms as operating in a space that is too risky to finance.

More often the problem is simply that asymmetry of information about the business opportunity between entrepreneurs and investors leads investors either to offer entrepreneurs too little capital or to offer that capital at too high a premium over the prevailing rate in financial markets. Information asymmetry between the entrepreneur and the investor leads the investor to face the risk of *moral hazard*, or behavior by the entrepreneur against the interests of the investor. For example, the investor might not know for sure whether the entrepreneur really needs a large number of company cars for the business to work effectively or whether the entrepreneur just wants to drive a free car. To protect themselves against this threat of moral hazard, investors might decide not to invest in certain ventures or to charge those ventures a premium to compensate for losses that the investors incurred in investing in the wrong ventures. Franchisees are willing to make these investments at a lower price than passive investors because, as owner-operators, they have a greater ability to monitor and gather information about the business than is the case for passive investors.

Some businesses are difficult to finance because they have limited fixed assets. Take cleaning businesses as an example. The primary assets in a cleaning business—things such as brand names and a set of operating procedures—are intangible. The effective use of intangible assets is much harder for investors to monitor than the effective use of tangible assets. Moreover, the difficulty of redeploying intangible assets to other uses gives them very low liquidation value.[9] Add that to the fact that collateral is scarce when tangible assets are not present, and you find that financing companies made up largely of intangible assets is quite difficult. Franchising, of course, mitigates this problem by providing firms with a capital transfer from outlet operators and by minimizing the amount of capital that firms need for their operations.

Franchising allows firms to raise capital at a cheaper price than is the case if they were to issue equity. One of the problems about the operation of businesses mentioned earlier is that outlet managers who earn straight salaries do not have strong incentives to work hard. This incentive problem means that investors in the shares of a chain of company-owned outlets expect to earn lower return on the shares that they hold than the outlet operators would earn if they owned the outlets themselves. Although the investment in the shares of the chain might be less risky than the investment in the individual outlets, the greater return that would come from franchising outweighs the benefits of diversification. As a result, franchisors can raise money more cheaply if they sell franchises to individual outlets than if they sell shares in the overall chain to investors and hire managers to operate the outlets.

Of course, there are also some nonfinancial advantages of franchising over raising debt or equity to finance growth. One option for small companies seeking to grow large is venture capital financing. Venture capital suffers from the drawback that it requires entrepreneurs to give up some amount of organizational control to their investors. Franchising, in contrast, allows capital to be acquired without giving up control of the company. Many entrepreneurs would prefer to retain full control over their companies when they finance them. In fact, research shows that 91 percent of entrepreneurs who decided to franchise chose that mode of business because of the loss of control that would come along with bringing on investors.[10]

Human Resource Acquisition

Not only is franchising an effective mechanism for obtaining the capital to grow a business, but it is also an effective mechanism for obtaining the human resources needed to grow. Establishing and operating business outlets is time consuming. Employees have to be hired and trained, equipment purchased and set up, and locations identified and leased or purchased. Franchising enhances firm growth by allowing the firm's management to specialize in identifying, selecting, and training franchisees, while leaving someone else the responsibility of hiring and supervising the employees who serve customers. Thus, firms that rely more on franchising tend to grow larger.

Figure 2.1 shows the relationship between the size of a chain in the number of outlets and the reliance on franchising. It indicates that larger chains have a greater reliance on franchising than smaller ones.

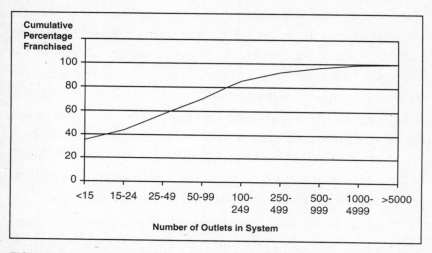

FIGURE 2.1   The Percentage of Franchised Outlets by Size of the System

Source: Adapted from data contained in R. Bond, *Bond's Franchise Guide*, (Oakland, CA: Sourcebook Publications, 2004).

Stop! Don't Do It!

1. Don't use company-owned outlets when you want to grow your business quickly.

2. Don't own all of your outlets if you want to overcome financial and human resource constraints on the growth of your firm.

A Lucrative Financial Model

Although providing incentives to managers and enhancing growth are important objectives for entrepreneurs and senior managers at many companies, the ultimate goal of these individuals is to enhance the profitability of their firms. Franchising is a valuable business model for companies because it is financially lucrative, providing a mechanism for reducing a company's risk while enhancing its returns on invested capital.

Risk Sharing

Franchising is a useful tool for passing off risk to another party. When a company franchises, its franchisees bear some of the financial risk that comes from adding outlets in new locations that might or might not be successful. If the capital that a firm uses to establish the new outlets belongs to franchisees, the risk of expansion is borne by the franchisees. Therefore, one way for a firm to manage risk is to franchise outlets in new locations and have the franchisees bear the risk of figuring out whether the new locations will be successful. When the value of particular locations is known, the franchisor can buy back the successful locations and leave the unsuccessful ones franchised. In fact, most franchisors tend to do just this, retaining the highest-performing outlets and franchising the lower-performing ones.

Not only will this franchising strategy help your company to manage risk, but it also will enhance the company's performance. Because some outlets always generate better returns than others, the financial performance of your company can be enhanced by shedding poor-performing outlets. By removing the poor-performing outlets from your financial statements, your numbers will improve. In fact, if you franchise, you can allow individual outlets to fail without adversely affecting the value of your equity position, which you cannot do with company-owned outlets. Thus, franchising is a tool for reducing the drag of poor-performing outlets on overall financial performance.

Franchising is an effective risk-management strategy for several other reasons as well. When outlets are all company-owned, chains earn their profits from the operation of their outlets. In contrast, when outlets are completely franchised, chains earn royalties on gross sales at outlets. The risk of a business is very much affected by the variance in performance. For two businesses with the same average performance, the risk is much higher in the one with more varied performance than in the one with more constant performance. Because variation in sales tends to be smaller than variation in profits, compensation through royalties is less risky than compensation through profits from operating a chain.

Moreover, firms can mitigate risk through diversification. By operating in a variety of different geographic markets where performance between outlets is uncorrelated, companies can reduce their risk. As long as sales and profit increases in one market are matched by sales and profit declines in another market, the overall performance of a firm will be stable, despite fluctuations in local markets. Because franchising allows firms to expand into broader geographic markets more quickly than if they own all of their own outlets, firms can diversify the risks of differences in the performance of companies across different geographic markets more effectively, allowing returns to occur at a lower level of risk.[11]

Franchising can also be used as a strategy to pass off risks of third parties, such as those of customer liability or those created by low-wage workers. By franchising, companies can make employment of workers in an outlet the responsibility of independent companies. Therefore, the kinds of problems that low-wage, part-time workers impose on a company can be passed off to someone else.[12] In addition, franchisors have limited liability for the injuries to customers in retail outlets; whereas the operators of company-owned outlets are liable for customer injuries on their premises.[13] Therefore, the risk of liability for customer injury—and the cost of insuring against it—can be transferred to another party through franchising.

Return on Investment (ROI)

An even more basic benefit of franchising to financial returns is that of its effect on return on investment. The financial return on an investment is composed of three key factors: the amount of capital invested to generate the return, the revenues resulting from that investment, and the costs of generating those revenues. In general, franchising generates a higher return on investment than is the case with ownership of outlets. In fact, PepsiCo franchised off many company-owned outlets of Pizza Hut® because the company wanted to generate a higher return on investment, and the capital that the firm had invested in owned outlets hindered that return.

Why is return on investment so much higher with franchising than with company ownership of outlets? Although the revenues garnered by a company through franchising tend to be lower than the revenues garnered through operating those outlets directly, these reduced revenues are accompanied by even lower costs. Compared to companies that operate chains of outlets directly, franchisors have relatively few employees per dollar of revenue, making their cost structure very low.

Moreover, franchisors spend far less to monitor outlet operators than do nonfranchising chains because the incentive effects of franchising are so large that franchisees do not need to be monitored as closely as company-owned outlet managers.[14] In fact, when using franchising, many companies find that the cost of monitoring outlets can be cut by as much as half of the cost of monitoring company-owned outlets.[15]

Franchise systems do not require much working capital, further reducing costs. In fact, because some franchisors even collect royalties weekly but pay their bills quarterly, franchising can generate negative working capital, making the cost of operations very low indeed.[16]

Franchising also requires a much smaller up-front investment to generate the same amount of operating profit as company ownership of outlets. Franchisors invest almost nothing in physical capital, with their investments in these assets being limited largely to computer and office equipment and the establishment of the systems—information technology, the development of an operations manual, training, and the prototype stores—that they need to support franchisees.[17] The costs to set up and run the outlets themselves—the building, equipment, advertising, and employees—are borne by the franchisees. Therefore, franchising generates a very high return on investment.

Stop! Don't Do It!

1. Don't use a business model of company-owned outlets if you want to minimize risk.

2. Don't use company-owned outlets if you want to generate high return on capital invested; by cutting investment and operating costs, franchising generates a high ROI.

Questions to Ask Yourself

1. Do I need to provide outlet managers with an incentive to self-select to get the best outlet operators?

2. Will my business benefit from strong incentives to minimize shirking by the managers of my outlets?

3. Do I need to grow my business rapidly to be competitive?

4. Do I need economies of scale in my business?

5. Can I obtain the capital and human resources that I need to grow through means other than franchising?

6. Do I want to pass off the risks and responsibilities of establishing retail outlets to another party rather than bearing them myself?

7. Do I want a business model that generates a high return on investment?

Summary

This chapter identified the three major advantages of franchising: providing better mechanisms for selecting and providing incentives to outlet operators; offering an efficient mechanism for obtaining human and financial resources for rapid firm growth; and providing a lucrative financial model, generating returns at relatively low risk. Franchising provides an effective mechanism for mitigating problems of adverse selection and shirking. By making the compensation of an outlet manager dependent on his or her ability and effort, franchising facilitates the self-selection of people with the right skills and motivation to operate the business profitably. It also minimizes the shirking of outlet operators by making their compensation directly dependent on how hard they work. This leads franchisees to work harder than salaried managers to generate sales, motivates them to control costs more carefully, and makes them more innovative.

Rapid growth is very important to many firms because it facilitates the cost-effective promotion of the company's brand name, allows for large-scale purchasing of inputs, lowers the average cost of developing key assets, and allows firms to lock up desirable geographic locations. Franchising makes it possible for firms to obtain capital quickly and cheaply because it passes off the major costs of outlet development to franchisees and overcomes information asymmetry problems in the market for venture capital. Moreover, by providing strong incentives for outlet operators to make operations profitable, franchising lowers the cost of accessing equity capital—and does so without requiring the entrepreneur to give up ownership and control over the business. Franchising allows companies to specialize in selling and managing franchises and franchisees to specialize in the provision of the product or service to end customers. This specialization, combined with the reduction in the adverse effects of hierarchy on information transmission, allows companies to grow large at a lower human resource cost than is the case with direct operation of outlets.

Franchising provides a lucrative financial model, generating high returns at relatively low risk. It provides a mechanism for passing off the risk of establishing new outlets to another party, as well as permitting a company to operate only the most lucrative outlets. Franchising also helps to minimize variance in performance by linking compensation to sales, which are more stable than profits. Furthermore, it facilitates the use of geographic diversification as a risk-management strategy.

Franchising generates a high return on investment. Because franchisors have lower costs than companies that operate their own outlets, they can often generate a higher per outlet profit margin than vertically integrated chains. Given the low level of up-front capital invested by franchisors—most of the capital investment to set up outlets is provided by franchisees—franchisors earn a higher return on capital invested than the operators of company-owned chains of outlets.

Now that you understand the major advantages of franchising, we turn to the major disadvantages of this mode of business, which are the subject of the next chapter.

3

THE DISADVANTAGES OF FRANCHISING

There is no such thing as a free lunch—not even at a franchised restaurant or fast food operation. The advantages of franchising described in the last chapter come at a cost. By comparing the costs of franchising described in this chapter with the benefits of franchising described in the last chapter, you can better decide whether franchising is worthwhile for your business. This will also help you figure out how to compete with other firms that use franchising.

Franchising creates four types of disadvantages for companies. Because franchising is based on written contracts between independent companies, it suffers from goal conflict between franchisors and franchisees that sometimes spills over into legal disputes. Franchising also creates several transaction cost problems, most notably free riding (discussed later in this chapter), that do not exist within company-owned chains. Franchising makes certain types of innovation and change difficult to execute because of the lack of control that franchisors have over the actions of their franchisees. Finally, under certain conditions, franchising might generate lower financial returns than company ownership of outlets.

Goal Conflict Between Franchisors and Franchisees

Franchising suffers from an inherent goal conflict between franchisors and franchisees. Because franchisors make money from royalties on gross sales, they seek to maximize the level of sales generated across all of their franchised outlets. In contrast, franchisees are compensated from profits on the outlets that they own and thus seek to maximize the level of profits at their outlets. Strategies that maximize system-wide sales and strategies that maximize profits at individual outlets are not the same, leading franchisors and franchisees to want to adopt different strategies.

Maximizing Sales versus Maximizing Profits

One effect of the franchisor's desire to maximize sales and the franchisee's desire to maximize profit is a conflict over whether to adopt high-volume, low-margin business strategies. In general, maximizing sales tends to occur at lower prices and at higher quantities than maximizing profits. Thus, franchisees tend to prefer strategies that involve selling a lower quantity at a higher price than their franchisors would like.[1]

This conflict manifests itself in disagreements between franchisors and franchisees over the product mix for the business. Take, for example, auto-repair franchises. Brake work might be a high-margin item, but it occurs at relatively low volume because of the relatively small number of customers that need their brakes repaired. In contrast, an oil change might be a much higher-volume item because of the need to change engine oil frequently. However, this activity might have a very narrow profit margin for the company providing the service. Franchisors in the auto-repair business would prefer to have their franchisees emphasize oil changes, while the franchisees would try hard to spend most of their time repairing brakes.

A related conflict occurs when franchisors try to encourage sales at outlets in their chains. A common way to increase sales is by offering customers a coupon to generate interest in the system's products. Franchisors almost always see the provision of coupons as a good idea because it increases sales and, hence, franchisor royalties. However, the use of coupons often increases costs along with sales because the company must provide the additional free or discounted items. The increase in sales and costs that comes from the use of coupons frequently means that the higher level of sales occurs at a lower profit per unit, leading the franchisee's profit to suffer. As a result, franchisees frequently oppose the use of coupons to increase sales that franchisors try to get them to adopt.

Conflict over Outlet Concentration

Franchisors and franchisees often disagree over the right level of outlet concentration in an area. Franchisors want to establish more outlets of a chain in a given geographic area than franchisees would like to see. Because it is often difficult to increase sales without adding additional units—think coffee shops here—chain operators might want to add an additional unit that would increase overall sales, even if the increased sales comes at the expense of profits generated at existing units. Because franchisors make their money from royalties on gross sales and bear relatively few costs from adding outlets, they tend to want to add outlets up to the point at which the maximum number of customers is served. The franchisor might even want to add outlets that are unprofitable if they add to the reputation of the system and enhance overall sales. This means that the franchisor would like to add outlets as long as the additional royalties from sales are greater than the costs of supervising the franchisees.

Franchisees do not want as many outlets in the system as franchisors would have. Franchisees are compensated from profits net of royalties and other costs. Therefore, they try to maximize outlet-level profits. Franchisees do not want to establish additional outlets if the new units will cannibalize some of their sales and, therefore, adversely affect their profits. As Figure 3.1 shows, the difference in franchisor and franchisee compensation generates a fundamental conflict between franchisors and franchisees over the desired number of outlets in a given market. As the figure demonstrates, the number of outlets in the market increases the revenues of the system, but at a declining marginal rate; whereas the costs of additional outlets increase at a constant rate. Franchisees want to have the number of outlets that corresponds to the maximum gap between revenues and costs, while the franchisors want the number of outlets with the highest level of revenue.

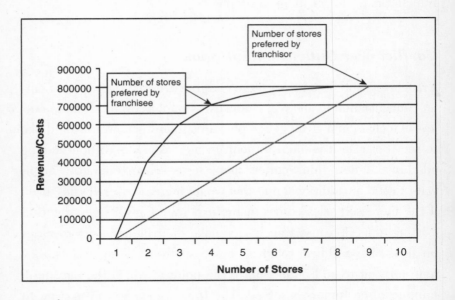

FIGURE 3.1 Franchisor and Franchisee Desired Levels of Outlet Concentration

The conflict between franchisors and franchisees over the concentration of outlets in a particular geographic market is often a major source of legal disputes between franchisors and franchisees, with many franchisees suing their franchisors over the establishment of new locations near their existing outlets. To reassure franchisees that they will not add outlets in a given geographic area, franchisors often grant franchisees exclusive territories, which are the subject of a more detailed discussion in Chapter 7, "Territorial Strategies."

Litigation between franchisors and franchisees and the adoption of policies to minimize the threat of litigation do not occur only when franchisors add new outlets. They also come from any effort by franchisors to deliver its product to end customers. For example, Pepsi® ended up in several disputes with its franchisees when it decided to offer its fast food products through supermarkets and other delivery mechanisms that competed with its outlets.

Regulators have also gotten involved in the issue of managing the problem of outlet concentration. As we will discuss in greater detail in Chapter 10, "The Legal and Institutional Environment for Franchising," some state governments, including Iowa's, have established laws to protect franchisees by precluding franchisors from establishing new outlets closer than 3 miles from any existing ones.

All of this makes litigation a much more prominent aspect of running a franchise system than is the case with a chain of company-owned outlets. In fact, conflict over outlet concentration and the level of litigation that surrounds it is one reason why some companies, such as Starbucks, are reluctant to franchise. When making the decision to franchise, you should consider the inevitable conflict that you will encounter with franchisees over outlet concentration if you choose to franchise.

Conflict over Collective Action

Franchising also has important disadvantages when a company wants to rely on collective action across outlets. Companies that own all of their own outlets do not care whether a particular outlet is advantaged or disadvantaged by a policy that the company adopts. Because the company will consolidate its financial statements across all outlets, its management is indifferent as to whether costs and revenues are balanced across outlets or whether some revenues are generated in one outlet as a result of costs incurred in another.

This is not so with franchised outlets. No franchisee is willing to undertake actions that would benefit the rest of the franchised chain but would harm his or her business. Therefore, policies undertaken in franchise systems need to ensure that they match costs and revenues at the outlet level. Because franchisees are independent companies, with their own shareholders and own financial statements, costs cannot be incurred in one location to support revenues generated in another location.

Take, for example, a warranty system for a chain of franchised auto-repair shops. Any warranty work performed by franchisees must be made equal to the amount of warranty claims made against a franchisee, or the franchisor and franchisees will end up in conflict. Franchisees do not want to have to perform more free warranty work than they are responsible for because of claims made against them. Because the customers are likely to have repair work under a warranty done somewhere other than the original shop where the claim was generated, the franchisor needs to compensate the franchisees doing the repairs, or they will not want a system-wide warranty policy. In particular, new franchisees will likely rebel against a system-wide warranty policy unless they are compensated for repair work. New franchisees will be the most adversely affected by the failure to compensate for repairs done under warranty because they will often be performing repairs under warranty for claims made against other franchisees without anyone else yet having to perform repairs on their work.[2]

Obsolescing Bargain

A final area of conflict between franchisors and franchisees lies in the temporal nature of the contributions of the two parties to the franchise system. Over time, the value to franchisees of the services and assets provided by the franchisor tends to shrink. While franchisees derive on-going value from the franchisor's effort to build the system brand name and from lower cost inputs that come from the exploitation of scale economies, much of the value that the franchisor provides to the franchisee dissipates over time. For instance, franchisees benefit from franchisor training and set-up assistance, but the value of these things declines after the franchisee has learned how to operate the outlet. The source of conflict lies in the fact that the royalty rate paid to the franchisor remains constant over time. Therefore, over time, franchisees begin to think that the royalties that they pay are too high, given the value that they derive from the system.

Stop! Don't Do It!

1. Don't franchise if you want a high density of outlets in a particular geographic area.
2. Don't franchise if your business depends heavily on collective action by operators of the different outlets.

Transaction Cost Problems

Because franchising involves the delivery of a product or service to end customers by a set of legally independent entities, it faces several transaction cost problems that are not present with chains of outlets owned by a single company. These include: free riding, hold-up, under-investment, and loss of intellectual property.

Free Riding

Franchisors develop a brand name and system for delivering a product or service to end customers; the delivery of the actual product or service is undertaken by legally independent entities—their franchisees. The fact that the franchisees are legally independent creates an important externality. Franchisees jointly use the brand name of the system. As a result, the cost of any one franchisee's actions to degrade the brand name is not borne completely by the degrading franchisee. Rather, it is borne by the entire chain. In contrast, any benefits that come from degrading the brand name—say, not paying the cost of ensuring an adequate level of customer satisfaction—is captured by the underinvesting franchisee. This externality creates an incentive for franchisees to free ride off the efforts of other franchisees.

Take, for instance, the case of oil change franchisees that do not replace oil filters, but merely clean them. If customers go to a franchisee that doesn't change oil filters properly, they develop a perception that the chain is of low quality and might stop frequenting the franchise system. The cost of the decreased demand that results is borne by all of franchisees in the system, proportional to the number of customers that they serve. However, the money saved by not replacing oil filters is captured by the single franchisee that does not replace the filters.

The incentive to free-ride is a disadvantage of franchising because it raises the cost of franchising. To combat free riding, franchisors must write quality standards into contracts and conduct audits to ensure that franchisees meet those standards. They also need to limit franchisee discretion by carefully specifying what franchisees can and cannot do. Take, for example, restaurant chefs. If franchisees have scripted menus and have to buy defined supplies directly from the franchisor, monitoring their behavior is easier. Scripted menus and set supplies reduce the opportunity for the chefs to make choices about ingredients that allow the substitution of inferior quality ingredients that degrade the brand name.

However, controlling the behavior of your franchisees is not easy. You aren't going to be able to anticipate everything that they could do; this makes it hard to write a complete contract that covers all possible contingencies. And whatever you don't write into the contract won't be covered.

Moreover, as a franchisor, you are limited in your control over franchisees. As will be discussed in greater detail in later chapters, you are limited in what you can dictate to your franchisees. For instance, you are not permitted to specify the prices at which products can be sold to end customers—you can only suggest prices.[3]

Franchisors often control franchisee free riding by designating suppliers. By dictating that franchisees use a certain source of supply, franchisors can minimize the potential for franchisee free riding by eliminating the option of substituting a lower-cost source of supply for the one recommended by the franchisor. If only some franchisees do this, the degradation of quality that results is borne by all outlets in the system, while the benefits of free riding are garnered by only those who substitute for cheaper supplies. Thus, those who substitute for lower-cost supplies gain at the expense of the rest of the system.

Unfortunately, antitrust laws hold that franchisors can dictate suppliers only when the supply is central to the product or brand of the company. For instance, KFC® can dictate to its franchisees who will be the supplier of the 11 herbs and spices in its chicken, but not who will be the supplier of plastic utensils. In addition to the fact that this arrangement increases the potential for franchisees to free-ride, there is another cost to franchisors. For supplies that are subject to volume discounts, such as the plastic utensils at KFC, there might be a significant cost savings in choosing one supplier. Therefore, centralized purchasing might have significant benefits to companies, which are lost if franchisors cannot dictate suppliers.[4]

The incentive to free-ride also leads franchisees to underinvest in advertising, compared to what the managers of a company-owned chain would invest on a per-outlet basis. Because advertising is an important mechanism to get customers into outlets, underinvesting in advertising leads to a lower level of sales in franchised chains than would be the case if free riding on advertising did not occur.

So why do franchisees underinvest in advertising? That question is best answered by looking at an example. Suppose you have opened a new subway sandwich franchise called Scott's Super Subs. As long as there is only one location in the media market, the franchisee of that location would have an incentive to advertise. The ads would generate increased demand for the subs and, therefore, enhance the performance of the outlet.

However, what if there was more than one franchised outlet in the media market? Then each of the franchisees has an incentive to underinvest in advertising. Regardless of who paid for the ad, customers would be attracted to the outlets. And they would probably go to the outlet nearest to them. Each of the franchisees would have an incentive to free-ride and save on the cost of the ad. If the other franchisees in town paid for the ad, the franchisee that didn't pay for it would still get additional customers.

To combat this problem, you, as a franchisor, need to write contracts with all of your franchisees to ensure that they make minimum advertising payments to support the development of the brand. Not only are these contracts difficult to write, but they are also costly to enforce. You need to write down in the franchise contract the conditions that the franchisee has to meet to comply with the advertising requirements. Given the cost of lawyers, the amount of money that this takes is not trivial.

Moreover, you need to reserve the right to terminate the franchisees if they don't comply with the terms, to ensure that the contract has teeth. That, of course, makes your franchisees concerned that you will use the efforts to control franchisee behavior as a way to take advantage of them, causing you more expense to reassure the franchisees that you will act in good faith.

Sometimes the threat of free riding means that companies simply give up on the idea of franchising altogether and replace franchisees with salaried managers. Because the operators of company-owned outlets do not get to keep any savings from failing to keep bathrooms clean or provide replacement auto filters, or underinvesting in advertising, or engaging in any of the other ways in which franchisees free ride, company-owned outlet managers do not have any reason to engage in this behavior. Without a reason, they do not do it—and the problem is avoided.

Hold-up

The previous section mentioned the concern of franchisees that franchisors will use the threat of termination to take advantage of them. This problem is a real one and is not to be taken lightly. Franchisors replace franchisees fairly regularly. In fact, the International Franchise Association conducted a study that showed that approximately 16 percent of all franchise outlets turn over every year. Moreover, as Table 3.1 shows, this turnover rate ranges from 10 percent to 51 percent across different industries.[5]

TABLE 3.1   Average Annual Outlet Turnover Rates for Selected Industries

Industry	Average Turnover Rate
Baked goods	50.5%
Printing and copying	19.4%
Fast food	19.0%
Maintenance services	16.2%
Services	16.1%
Retail food	15.9%
Education related	15.7%
Business services	14.4%
Travel	14.2%
Auto repair	13.4%
Building and construction	12.4%
Lodging	12.3%
Child related	12.1%
Personnel services	12.1%
Real estate	11.9%
Restaurants	11.1%
Retail	10.7%
Sports and recreation	10.4%
Overall	**16.0%**

Source: Adapted from data contained in the IFA Educational Foundation's *The Profile of Franchising* (Washington, D.C.: IFA, 1998).

The high rate of turnover of franchised outlets is important because it raises the fear that franchisees have of termination by opportunistic franchisors seeking to take advantage of them. Franchisees have to make investments in assets that are highly specific to the franchise system that they are entering, whether those investments are in signs, distinctive buildings, proprietary machines, or other things. In fact, one study showed that the average franchisee has to invest approximately $144,000 in assets that are specific to the franchise system in just the first year after buying an outlet.[6]

These large investments in assets that are specific to the franchise system, combined with the right of franchisors to terminate franchisees, creates the opportunity for franchisors to engage in something called *hold-up*. Hold-up occurs when one party takes advantage of another party's investment in specific assets to extract money from the second party. For example, suppose that an eye-care franchise has specially designed equipment for making its brand of eye glasses. The franchisor could opportunistically renegotiate with the franchisees to get them to pay additional royalties by threatening to terminate the franchisees or by refusing to approve the sale of the franchisee's outlet to another franchisee. Once the franchise agreements were terminated, the franchisees would be precluded from using the equipment specific to the franchise system. As long as the cost of replacing the equipment was more than cost of the additional royalties that the franchisees would have to pay the franchisor, the franchisees would likely consent to pay the additional royalties.

Although threatening termination is a common way for franchisors to hold up franchisees, it is not the only way that franchisors act opportunistically to appropriate some of the returns to the franchisee's investment in the system. Take, for example, the case of Fotomat®, a film-distribution franchisor. Having discovered that it earned much higher profits from company-owned outlets than it had expected and that it had sold its franchises at too low a fee, Fotomat established company-owned outlets near the locations of its franchised outlets and ended the film pickup and delivery services it had offered its franchisees. This set of actions cut the level of profits at the franchised outlets and allowed Fotomat to buy them back at a discount.[7]

Consider another example, this one of a car-rental franchise that had set up an outlet just outside of a major airport. The franchisor and franchisee agreed that the franchisee would pay 5 percent of sales as royalties in return for the use of the brand name and participation in the national reservation system. The franchisor then opportunistically sought a royalty rate increase to 7 percent of sales by threatening to add another franchise on the other side of the airport.[8] Because the franchisee realized that his sales would be cut almost in half by the establishment of another franchise near the same airport, he accepted the royalty rate increase.

Under Investment

Another disadvantage with franchising is that it can lead to underinvestment by franchisees. In comparison to a large retail chain that can raise money through financial markets, such as Starbucks, the individual purchasers of franchises, who invest a large portion of their net worth in a single outlet, tend to be undiversified. This lack of diversification leads them to view investment in the development of the outlet as riskier than the diversified owners view the same investment. As a result, franchisees are less willing to make those investments or are willing to make them only for a higher rate of return than diversified corporations, leading to underinvestment in outlets through franchising.[9]

Loss of Intellectual Property

In many retail businesses, the heart of the business's competitive advantage lies in its intellectual property. This intellectual property could be the firm's method of operations, as is the case with Merry Maids® cleaning service, or it could be the firm's equipment, as is the case with East Coast Original Frozen Custard®'s frozen dessert machines. Regardless of the form that the intellectual property takes, an intellectual property–based competitive advantage makes franchising problematic.

The first issue is that of disclosure. To franchise, the franchisor must provide the franchisee with the intellectual property that provides the competitive advantage to the business. Unless the intellectual property is patented, efforts to transfer this type of competitive advantage to franchisees are problematic. To get potential franchisees to buy your intellectual property, you need to show them why that intellectual property is valuable. However, your efforts to convince the franchisee of the value of your intellectual property demonstrate what that intellectual property does, thereby allowing them to imitate your intellectual property without paying for it. [10]

The second issue concerns trade secrecy, which is difficult to maintain through franchising. For trade secrets to be preserved, efforts must be taken to keep the secrets secret. The best way to do this is not to put the secret into the public domain. Unfortunately, this is not possible in franchising. Franchisees need to gain access to many of your company's trade secrets to operate their outlets. Therefore, as a franchisor, you have to rely on nondisclosure agreements to preserve your trade secrets. However, the use of nondisclosure agreements to control behavior faces strong limitations when the secret is being given to hundreds, if not thousands, of franchisees. The more people who have access to information, the greater is the likelihood that the information will leak out, even if you sign nondisclosure agreements with the recipients.

Furthermore, trade secrets often work best when the knowledge underlying them is tacit and hard to write down. However, franchising requires the codification of operations in operating manuals given to franchisees. Although most franchisors require franchisees to return the system's operating manual if they leave the system, the fact that the operations have been written down in the manual and the manual has been given to others makes it very difficult for franchisors to ensure that trade secrets contained in the operating manual are kept secret.

Take, for example, the difficulty that East Coast Original Frozen Custard has in protecting its proprietary custard and yogurt mixes, which are its primary competitive advantage. The chemical composition of these mixes is what gives the company's product its distinctive flavor. The company's franchise agreement bars franchisees from conducting analysis of the mixes to determine their chemical composition. However, this legal barrier is relatively weak; by operating an East Coast Custard franchise, people would have the opportunity to figure out the composition of the mixes and create duplicative products.

Stop! Don't Do It!

1. Don't franchise when the threat of free riding on quality or advertising is high; you are better off with company-owned outlets under these conditions.

2. Don't franchise when the threat of franchisor hold-up through adding nearby outlets or other means is high; you will have difficulty getting franchisees.

3. Don't franchise when your key competitive advantages are trade secrets that are easily imitated.

Innovation and Change

Franchising is not the most effective organizational form if a business needs to engage in certain types of innovation and change. Specifically, it tends to be ineffective when organizations need to change their structure frequently. In addition, franchising is problematic when an organization wants to test particular innovations to the system, as well as to transfer those innovations from one outlet to another.

Making Changes to Structure

Franchising is a poor choice of an organizational arrangement if you want to have the flexibility to change organizational structure regularly. To change organizational structure, franchisors must change their contracts with franchisees—and contracts with franchisees are difficult to alter. Unlike internal organizational structure and employment relationships that are used to manage the relationships between outlets in a company-owned chain, which can be changed at will, relationships between franchised outlets are set out in formal contracts that are governed by contract laws. Changing these relationships means renegotiating legal agreements. Not only does this effort incur substantial legal costs, but most franchisees also are unwilling to accept changes to organizational arrangements unless these changes benefit them. As a result, a franchisor that has discovered that it provides franchisees with, say, too many services might not be able to change the contractual provisions regarding services provided to franchisees.

Moreover, as will be described in greater detail in Chapter 10, in many states, any material change in the franchise relationship requires changes in franchise documents filed with state regulators.[11] Thus, changing the franchise relationship requires regulatory review as well as the administrative costs of making the changes to all documents provided to franchisees.

As a franchisor, you also cannot make changes to your system in a piecemeal fashion. Unlike with company-owned stores, where managers or entrepreneurs can give some outlets the best support and training and starve others of resources, in franchising, outlets have to be treated equally. Franchise discrimination laws make it difficult to treat new franchisees differently from existing franchisees. This makes it very difficult to establish new provisions in franchise contracts. Without the option of providing new terms to new franchisees, franchisors must get all of their franchisees to accept a change to alter their structures.

Franchising is very ineffective in business settings in which developments that could not be foreseen at the time of the writing of the original franchise contracts have a powerful effect on an industry, for many of the same reasons as those discussed earlier. The most notable example of this lies in information technology. Many franchisors have had difficulty requiring franchisees to adopt computers to provide point-of-sale information. Their contracts—written before the widespread adoption of computers—do not have any language about technology use. In contrast to the case with company-owned locations, franchisors cannot force their franchisees to adopt this technology if it was not foreseen and written into the agreements.[12]

Similarly, franchising inhibits efforts to examine the potential of future product offerings. Take, for example, an ice cream shop. A franchisor might consider offering cookies as a way to increase sales. To sell cookies, the outlet would need space set aside for baking and the installation of an oven. The allocation of this space and the expenses of installing an oven are worthwhile only if the ice cream shop actually sells cookies. If not, the space and equipment are wasted.

With a company-owned outlet, the firm can design the outlet to sell only ice cream and change it later to experiment with cookie sales. During the time when only ice cream is sold, the design of the outlet is optimal for the products being sold. With franchising, however, the outlet must be initially designed with the oven set-up present, even if this is not optimal before cookies are being sold. It is simply too difficult to introduce changes to the franchise system that are not initially established in the franchise contract.

Product Innovation

Franchising is also a relatively ineffective model for organizations that seek to develop and introduce new products frequently. One problem that franchisors face is a lack of information necessary to develop new products and services effectively. Many innovative new products are developed by research and development departments based on information about customer preferences and demand provided by marketing departments. However, because franchisees are independent companies, the quality of the marketing information that they transmit to franchisor headquarters for the purposes of developing new products is much worse than that provided by company-owned outlets. Only company-owned operations provide real-time management-information systems to gather up-to-date data on what is going in the outlets. The legal independence of franchisees, combined with the requirement that franchisees pay royalties on gross sales, makes most franchisees reluctant to provide franchisors with real-time information about their operations. Therefore, the management of a franchised chain has less marketing information to use to develop new products than it would if it operated its own outlets. As a result, companies are much better able to generate new products if they own their outlets than if they franchise them.

Another problem with innovation in franchise organizations is that it is difficult for franchisors to get franchisees to adopt new products that the franchisor developed. Getting franchisees to agree to changes is a slower and more time-consuming process than getting the managers of company-owned outlets to agree to the same changes. This is because franchisors have no direct authority over the behavior of franchisees the way that managers have authority over the behavior of their employees. Employment contracts allow managers to tell their employees what to do even if the employees disagree with them. However, franchising contracts do not allow entrepreneurs and managers to tell franchisees what to do. Therefore, as many franchisors have aptly pointed out, you can tell employees what to do, but you have to sell franchisees to get them to do what you want.[13]

The requirement that franchisors use persuasion rather than command and control to effect change in their organizations makes change slower to accomplish and more likely to fail. Take, for example, Pizza Hut's difficulty of persuading franchisees to accept home delivery. Many franchisees simply refused to adopt this innovation when it was first introduced, despite the many hours spent by the management of Pizza Hut to try to persuade them.

The level of knowledge transfer from one franchisee to another is also low in comparison to knowledge transfer between company-owned outlets. Because communication patterns and incentives to work together are very low between companies that are owned by different individuals, franchisees have little reason or opportunity to share information, relative to the managers of outlets in a chain of company-owned outlets. In a study of pizza franchises, for example, professors Eric Darr, Linda Argote, and Dennis Epple found that franchisees were less likely to transfer knowledge about their innovations to other franchisees than the managers of company-owned outlets were to transfer knowledge to other outlets.[14]

Stop! Don't Do It!

1. Don't use franchising if you want the flexibility to change organizational structure frequently.
2. Don't use franchising if frequent new product introduction is important to your business.

Financial Returns

The previous chapter pointed out many of the financial benefits of franchising, but there are also several financial costs to franchising. The first of these costs is that of establishing a franchise system, which estimates suggest can exceed $500,000.[15] The up-front cost of franchising is important because it makes your analysis of whether you should franchise highly dependent on the number of outlets that you plan to have in your system. If you plan to establish a large chain, this up-front cost will be amortized over a large number of units, making its impact on your overall operations trivial. However, if you plan to franchise only a handful of outlets, the benefits of franchising might be overwhelmed by the basic cost of setting up the system, leading you to conclude that franchising isn't really worthwhile. Table 3.2 illustrates the effect of franchise system size on the economics of franchising versus company ownership of outlets.

TABLE 3.2 Balancing the Costs and Benefits of Franchising and Company Ownership

	Franchising	Company Ownership
Cost of establishing the system	$500,000	$0
Sales per outlet	$400,000	$350,000
Profits per outlet per year	$0	$35,000
Royalties per outlet per year	$20,000	$0
Capital cost per outlet	$0	$200,000
Up-front fee per outlet	$10,000	$0
Earnings on 5 outlets over 10 years	$550,000	$750,000
Earnings on 10 outlets over 10 years	$1,600,000	$1,500,000

In the hypothetical example in Table 3.2, franchising is much less profitable than company ownership if the chain has only five franchisees because of the high up-front cost to set up the system. On the other hand, franchising is more profitable than company ownership of outlets once the chain has ten outlets because the financial benefits of having the capital costs paid by franchisees and the benefits of receiving the up-front fees (that were discussed in the last chapter) overtake the effects of the up-front cost of setting up the system.

Another cost that you want to consider when evaluating the advantages and disadvantages of franchising is that chains of company-owned outlets tend to generate greater amounts of profit per outlet than franchised ones. Why? Franchisors earn royalties only on gross sales, and the royalty rate is often less than the margins earned by the outlet operator. Take, for example, ABRA Auto Body & Glass, a collision-repair franchise out of Brooklyn Center, Minnesota. The average outlet in this system earns 9.7 percent of sales before taxes, while franchisor royalties are 5 percent of sales.[16] Thus, in this case, the franchisor is taking about one-third of the margins and giving two-thirds to the franchisee.

Stop! Don't Do It!

1. Don't franchise if you plan to operate a very small chain; the up front costs of setting up the system will not be recouped.

2. Don't forget to consider the relative margins generated by company-ownership of outlets and franchising in calculating the financial returns to franchising.

Questions to Ask Yourself

1. Can I avoid competing with my franchisees through operations at my own outlets?

2. Do I have something (brand name) that will maintain its value to franchisees over time and justify ongoing royalties?

3. Can I control franchisee free riding?

4. Can I reassure franchisees that I will not take advantage of their investments in my system?

5. Can I protect my intellectual property against disclosure to competitors while still licensing it to others?

6. Can I contractually agree to the products and services to be sold and the organizational form of the business for years at a time?

7. How do financial returns from franchising and company ownership compare in my business? Which one is really better for the type and size of operation I am creating?

Summary

This chapter identified the four major disadvantages of franchising: goal conflict between franchisors and franchisees; transaction cost problems, such as free riding, that exist in franchising but not within company-owned chains; the difficulty engaging in innovation and change in franchised organizations; and lower absolute profits from franchising, as compared to company ownership of outlets.

Franchising suffers from an inherent goal conflict between franchisors and franchisees because franchisors earn royalties on gross sales of their systems, and franchisees make profits net of royalties at individual outlets. Franchisors seek lower prices and higher volume of sales than franchisees. They want a higher level of outlet density in a given geographical area than franchisees. Franchisees are often unwilling to engage in collective actions because they gain only if their particular outlets benefit from a policy. Finally, the value to franchisees of being part of a franchise system declines as they become more experienced, causing conflict with franchisors who maintain their royalty rates at a constant level.

Because franchisors and franchisees are legally independent entities, franchising suffers from several transaction cost problems that are not present with chains owned and operated by a single entity. Franchisees have an incentive to free-ride off the efforts of other franchisees to uphold the brand name of the system. Franchisees worry that franchisors will opportunistically renegotiate the terms of the contract after the franchisees have invested in system-specific assets and appropriate franchisee profits. Franchisees also underinvest in outlets in comparison to the level of diversified shareholders in company-owned chains. Finally, franchising is a poor mode of business for protecting unpatented intellectual property, such as trade secrets.

Franchising is not a very effective form of organization if a business needs to innovate and change frequently. The use of contracts to govern relationships between franchisors and franchisees makes it difficult to change policies or structure, or adopt products or processes that were not known and specified in the agreement at the time that it was signed. Moreover, the lack of information about customer demand at franchised locations, combined with the lack of franchisor authority over franchisees, means that franchisors lack much of the information necessary to innovate and have trouble getting franchisees to adopt franchisor innovations after they have been developed.

Finally, franchising imposes several financial costs on franchisors. The first is the up-front cost associated with establishing a franchise system, which does not make franchising a cost-effective organizational form if a company franchises only a handful of outlets. The second is that franchising generates lower profits per outlet than company ownership, making it possible for firms to earn much more money by operating outlets directly rather than by franchising them.

Now that you understand the major disadvantages of franchising, the next chapter turns to a discussion of what business concepts can be franchised.

4

What Business Concepts Can Be Franchised?

To franchise a business successfully, you need a business concept that is appropriate. Unfortunately, many entrepreneurs and managers have tried unsuccessfully to sell franchises for business concepts for which franchising doesn't work very well. For example, franchising doesn't work well in the grocery business because the profit margins are too narrow to support royalty payments. Similarly, franchising doesn't work well for heating contractors because much of the expertise that companies have in this area cannot be written down and instead resides in the heads of company personnel.

In general, three factors make a business appropriate for franchising: The business is based on a proven system for serving end customers; that system can be reduced to a set of operating rules that can be transmitted to others in written form; and there are enough potential buyers of the concept to make it worthwhile to invest in the up-front costs of setting up a franchise system. This chapter offers specific information to help you assess how these three factors influence the appropriateness of your business concept for franchising. We begin with the value of the system.

Valuable System to Sell

To franchise, you must have a valuable system for providing a product or service to end customers. Although this might sound obvious, it turns out that this screen is one that many would-be franchisors fail to pass through. Most would-be franchisors cannot franchise because they do not have a valuable system for serving end customers.

What is a valuable system for serving end customers? It is not just having a product or service that customers want. Rather, it includes an operation for delivering that product or service to customers that is better than what potential franchisees would be able to develop if they started their own businesses from scratch. After all, there is no reason for franchisees to pay you good money for your business if you cannot provide them with a system that is better than the one they could develop on their own.

Developing a system that is better than the one that potential franchisees could develop by starting their own businesses depends in large part on having worked your way up the learning curve for running outlets. By doing things such as serving customers, purchasing raw materials, and making products, you get better at those activities. As Figure 4.1 illustrates, if you operate a prototype outlet for a while before franchising and refine the methods of producing and delivering your products and services, you are likely to come up with a system that is more efficient and effective than that available to potential franchisees at the time they are thinking of starting their businesses.

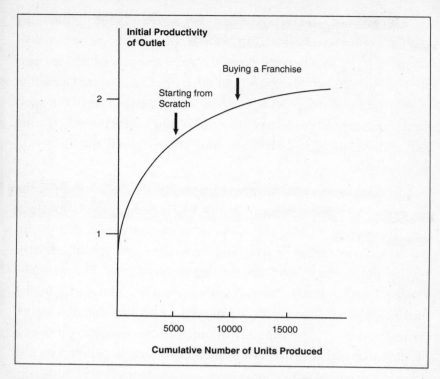

FIGURE 4.1   The Learning Curve Benefits of Franchising

Because one of the keys to developing a system that is valuable to franchisees is moving up the learning curve at operating outlets in your industry, there is a strong positive relationship between the length of time that franchisors have operated businesses before franchising and their ability to franchise their business concepts. For example, Blimpie® Subs and Salads, a fast food franchisor out of Atlanta, Georgia, has a business model that can be franchised in large part because it operated for 13 years as a company-owned restaurant chain before beginning to franchise. During this time, the owners of the company developed products, tested them with customers, figured out procedures for operating the outlets, and otherwise got the system to the point that they had something to sell to franchisees.

Moreover, operating a business for a while before franchising enables you to standardize your system. To franchise your business, you need to be able to write down the rules and procedures to operate the business, as well as to train others in that system. Operation of your business will provide you with an understanding of the standard processes and procedures that make your business work. Having this understanding will facilitate your ability to sell the system to other people.

Another aspect of a business that makes it worth buying is the possession of a proprietary product or a proprietary process for making that product. Having a proprietary advantage means that potential franchisees cannot provide end customers with your product or service unless they buy into the franchise system. For example, Dippin' Dots®, a frozen dessert franchisor out of Paducah, Kentucky, provides its franchisees with a patented technology for making ice cream "pellets".[1] The Dippin' Dots process is necessary to produce a product that meets customer demand for ice cream pellets, creating value in the company's system.

Another thing that makes a system worth buying is having a brand name that offers the franchise buyer a way to attract end customers. Brand names attract customers and make them more likely to purchase products or services than they would if the products or services were not associated with the brand name. For instance, Sylvan Learning Centers, an educational service center out of Baltimore, Maryland, has developed a strong brand name that attracts customers, making its system worth franchising. In fact, brand names are so beneficial that a strong brand name might attract enough customers to make it worthwhile to buy a franchise even if the franchisor offers no other benefit over starting an independent company.

Of course, a brand name helps a franchisor only if that brand name is protected. If other firms can copy the brand name easily, that brand name isn't going to be of much value to franchisees. Therefore, to have a business concept that works for franchising, a business needs to have a registered trademark, as well as defined signs, trade appearance, slogans, and so forth.[2] For this reason, franchisors register their trademarks and service marks, and develop a consistent trade appearance. For instance, East Coast Original Frozen Custard, of Solon, Ohio, has registered a service mark covering the use of that name for restaurant services that involve frozen desserts and a trademark on its name for the sale of frozen desserts, including custard, yogurt, shakes, and sundaes.

Although having a valuable operating system and brand name are important to making a business appropriate for franchising, they are not enough. The business must also have enough of a profit margin to allow franchisees to earn a return after royalties paid to the franchisor that exceeds the outlet manager's wage. Of course, this means that the best businesses to franchise are those that have very high margins, thereby ensuring that the profits franchisees earn after they pay royalties to franchisors are quite robust. For instance, the Golden Corral® Family Steakhouse, a restaurant chain out of Raleigh, North Carolina, indicates that average monthly net operating income at its franchised restaurants is 24.12 percent after the 4 percent royalty and 2 percent advertising fee on gross sales are paid.[3] This high net operating income shows that Golden Corral has enough of a margin on its operations to support a franchised operation.

Stop! Don't Do It!

1. Don't try to franchise a business if you haven't developed anything that makes buying into your business better than starting a business from scratch.

2. Don't try to franchise a business concept that you haven't proven by operating your own outlets for a while.

Transferable Concept

Having a valuable business system is only part of what you need to have a business concept that you can franchise. You also need a business concept that you can transfer easily to others. What does that mean? Basically, it means three things. You need to have a business concept that is easy to replicate. You also need to be able to reduce the operation of your business to written rules and procedures. Furthermore, you need to be able to teach people without experience in your business to operate the business in a short period of time by simply following those rules and procedures. If you can do all of these things, you probably have a business concept that you can franchise.

Replicable Concept

To franchise a business, you need a concept that is replicable. It has to be possible for someone to produce the same products or services and provide the same customer experience in more than one location. Otherwise, you won't be able to assure customers that your brand name represents a standard experience. For instance, if you have a business concept for a fresh scallop restaurant that relies on your ability to get access to Digby scallops every morning, you will have a real problem replicating your concept much beyond the bounds of Digby, Nova Scotia. On the other hand, the business concept of selling people a burger and fries is quite easily replicated. You can create outlets that use the same supplies and serve the same products in the same type of atmosphere in a wide variety of places in the world.

Concept That Can Be Codified

To franchise, you also need a business concept that can be reduced to written rules and procedures. Codification is important for several reasons. One of them is that the people operating the outlet have to be able to figure out the right decisions to make to operate your business without involving you and the other people who developed the business concept. For example, if you want to franchise your sub shop business concept, and that concept is based on using freshly baked bread, you need to be able to write down the recipe and procedures for making that bread so your franchisees can bake that bread without you getting involved. If you have to get involved in every decision that your franchisees make, your time will quickly get exhausted as your system grows, and your franchise operation will fail. To succeed, the method that the founders would have used for making specific decisions has to be something that franchisees can look up in an operating manual.

The ability to write down the operating rules and procedures for the business is also important because franchising is a business built around contracts. As a franchisor, you will sell your franchisees the rights to use your system's brand name and operating procedures. You will manage the franchisees by comparing their activities to rules and obligations set out in the franchise agreement. This means that the franchisee's obligations, the system's standards of quality and performance, the services and assistance to be offered to franchisees, and the procedures for managing employees all need to be codified. Otherwise, there will be no way to enforce the franchise contracts.

Moreover, as will be discussed further in Chapter 10, "The Legal and Institutional Environment for Franchising," franchising requires the codification of a business system because that is a necessary condition of regulatory approval. In the states requiring the registration of franchise systems, regulators will not allow franchisors to sell undefined operating systems, thereby making codification a precondition to selling a business concept as a franchisor.

Writing an operating manual and set of rules and procedures for a franchise might be the most difficult thing a franchisor ever does, but the ability to do so demonstrates that a business concept is appropriate for franchising. For instance, USA Baby, a retailer of children's furniture out of Elmhurst, Illinois, has codified the necessary steps for store design, merchandising, and customer service in this business. This enables USA Baby to write contracts with other parties to sell them this information, thereby allowing them to franchise.

If you are thinking of franchising a business, you should try to write an operating manual for your business. If you can't do it, that is a signal to you that you might not want to try franchising. There is no way for you to franchise your business if it can't be reduced to a set of rules put down in an operating manual.

Teachable Concept

Finally, to franchise you need to be able to teach your business concept to other people who do not have a lot of expertise in your industry in a relatively short period of time. Often this means that your business concept needs to be simple and something that can be implemented without great difficulty. The concepts cannot be hard to teach and cannot require a great deal of background knowledge to learn. Otherwise, your pool of potential franchisees will be too narrow for you to set up a successful chain of franchised outlets.

For instance, a chain of mental health clinics is not a very good business to franchise. To provide mental health assistance, people need to have a great deal of professional training. Without adequate time devoted to psychological training provided to people with the right background, you will not be able to produce franchisees capable of running a mental health clinic. In contrast, pretty much anyone can learn how to clean offices in a couple of weeks, making an office-cleaning business a much better bet for franchising than a mental health clinic.

To franchise, you also need to have figured out a way to teach the concept. Whether that training will be on-site or at your headquarters, you cannot franchise your business unless you can teach other people to run your business. Therefore, to franchise, you need to have developed a system for getting across the key concepts to operate your business to people who are buying the business from you. For example, TechZone® Airbag Service, a franchisor out of Mercer Island, Washington, has developed a system for airbag system repair that can be taught to franchisees in three weeks. The knowledge of how to repair airbags—in terms of both preopening and opening training—that TechZone Airbag Service provides is an important part of what makes the business appropriate for franchising.

Stop! Don't Do It!

1. Don't try to franchise a business concept if you cannot write down its operating rules and procedures.

2. Don't try to franchise a business concept if you cannot create an exact replica of your prototype outlet.

3. Don't try to franchise a business unless you know how to train other people with little expertise in your industry to operate your business in a short period of time.

Large Pool of Potential Franchisees

To franchise a business, you need to sell other people the business system that you developed. No matter how good your business concept is, and no matter how much profit people will make from exploiting your business concept, only some portion of the population is interested in running their own businesses and could potentially buy into your system. Couple that with the fact that you can persuade only some portion of the people interested in having their own businesses to buy your business concept (no matter how good a salesperson you are), and you will realize that, to sell franchises, you need a large pool of potential franchisees.

You get a large pool of potential franchisees for your concept if you come up with a concept that requires relatively little education, relatively little investment, and relatively little knowledge of an industry. Because more people can buy a franchise that meets these criteria than one that requires a lot of education, a large investment, and a great deal of industry knowledge, the ability to franchise your business concept depends on the number of people who could potentially buy it, all other things being equal.

Take, for instance, the concept underlying Carvel Ice Cream Factory, a frozen custard franchise out of Atlanta, Georgia. This business concept can be franchised to a very large number of potential franchisees. With an up-front franchise fee of only $10,000 and a minimum franchisee net worth requirement of only $100,000, a large number of people have the financial wherewithal to become Carvel Ice Cream franchisees. In addition, the operation of an ice cream shop is simple enough that a large percentage of the population can learn to operate it—no special education or industry experience is necessary.[4] Therefore, the ability of Carvel's founders to sell franchises to its frozen custard is greater than the ability of the founders of many business concepts to franchise their businesses.

Stop! Don't Do It!

1. Don't try to franchise a business concept if a large portion of the population does not have the money or skills to exploit the concept.

Questions to Ask Yourself

1. Is there demonstrated demand for the product or service that my business provides?

2. Do I have a working economic model that would provide franchisees with significant margins after paying royalties?

3. Do I have a proprietary method of operation that competitors cannot easily duplicate?

4. Do I have a distinctive brand name with registered trademarks?

5. Can I provide ongoing services to franchisees over a long period of time?

6. Do I have a prototype outlet that has been tested, that has been shown to work, and that can be replicated?

7. Can I reduce my business to a written operating manual and teach people to operate my business from it without my direct assistance?

8. Can I write down franchisee obligations, standards of quality and performance, services and assistance to be offered to franchisees, and procedures for managing employees?

Summary

This chapter identified three factors that make a business concept appropriate for franchising: It is based on a valuable system for serving end customers that can be reduced to a set of operating rules, that can be transmitted to others in written form, and for which there are enough potential buyers of the concept to make it worthwhile to invest in the up-front costs of setting up a franchise system. To be successful at franchising, you need to make sure that your business concept matches up well against these three criteria.

Having a valuable system to sell to others means having a business that is better for a potential franchisee to buy than they can get by starting their own business from scratch. This value comes from having moved up the learning curve by operating the business for a while and having figured out the necessary products and processes to serve customers in your industry. It also means having standardized the system that you have developed. Preferably, this standardized system offers a proprietary advantage to franchisees that enables them to serve end customers in ways that competitors cannot. However, even without a proprietary advantage, you can have a valuable system if you offer franchisees something, such as a brand name, that brings in end customers. If all of these conditions are met and your franchisees could make a high enough profit margin after paying royalties to earn a decent return on their investment of time and money in the system, you have a valuable system to sell.

In addition to having a valuable system to sell to franchisees, you need to have a transferable concept. You cannot franchise a business concept unless that concept is easy to replicate across multiple outlets. The concept also needs to be reduced to written rules and procedures. Finally, the concept needs to be something that you can teach to other people without experience in your business in a short period of time.

A third dimension that makes a business concept appropriate for franchising is that it can be pursued by a large number of people. Because only a small percentage of the population will be interested in buying franchises, and you will want to be able to select among potential franchisees, you need to have a concept that does not require franchisees to have a great deal of education, industry knowledge, or investment capital. Otherwise, you will simply not find enough potential franchisees for your business.

Now that you understand what business concepts can be franchised, we turn to a discussion of the right policies and procedures for franchising, which are the subject of the next chapter.

5

KEY FRANCHISING POLICIES

Successful franchising requires adopting the right policies for managing the franchise system. My research on new franchise systems shows that close to three quarters of all new franchise systems fail within ten years of their start at franchising. In a way, these dismal statistics are heartening. Many of these failures can be attributed to the adoption of inappropriate or ineffective policies, particularly policies that are inappropriate for the system's size or age.[1] Although failure rates are high, we know what franchisors are doing wrong. You can increase your business's performance at franchising by adopting the right policies for managing your franchise system.

This chapter discusses the specific policies to adopt to make your franchise system successful. These policies can be broken down easily into four categories:

1. The appropriate rules toward ownership of franchised outlets

2. The right mechanisms to ensure that franchisees act in the best interest of the franchise system

3. The correct term for a franchise agreement, as well as its possible renewal

4. The appropriate policies for advertising, both national and local

Ownership of Franchised Outlets

One major policy decision that you need to address when setting up your franchise system is whether to allow *passive ownership*. Franchisors can require franchisees to operate their outlets directly or allow them to hire employees to manage their outlets for them; that is, they can permit passive ownership.

Passive ownership is fairly common in franchising. Only 24 percent of franchisors require franchisees to be owner-operators.[2] An example of a company that allows passive ownership is direct-mail advertising franchisor Trimark, out of Wilmington, Delaware.[3] Trimark allows passive ownership because of its focus on multiunit franchising, an arrangement in which a franchisor contracts with a franchisee that operates more than one unit (more information about multiunit franchising is provided in the next chapter).

Passive ownership sometimes makes sense when franchisors use it to support multiunit franchising because passive ownership makes possible two key advantages of that arrangement. It is often cheaper for an existing franchisee to add additional outlets than for the outlet to be sold to a new franchisee because the existing franchisee's experience allows the franchisor to cut training costs relative to what would be needed for a brand new franchisee. To allow existing franchisees to add units to their systems, the franchisor must permit passive ownership of the new outlets. In addition, multiunit franchising helps to reduce the problems of free riding. When franchisees own multiple outlets in a particular market, they tend to free-ride less than if they own only one outlet in a market. If a franchisee owns a large percentage of outlets in a market, he or she will gain less from free riding than if he or she owns a small percentage of the outlets because there will be fewer other parties onto whom to pass costs. Take, for example, free riding on advertising. If a franchisee owns all of the outlets in a particular media market, there is no benefit from free riding on advertising. All of the costs and benefits of advertising in that market go directly to the franchisee. There is no one on whom to free-ride.

Multiunit franchising is not the major reason that franchisors allow passive ownership, however. The most common reason for a passively owned franchise is that the franchisee is a wealthy individual who purchased the franchise as an investment. (The stereotypical example is a wealthy doctor or dentist.) Because the franchisee treats the franchise as an investment vehicle, devoting some of his or her portfolio toward purchasing the franchise rather than buying real estate, stocks, or bonds, he or she does not operate the outlet and hires someone else to do that.

Passive ownership is very common in franchising, but research shows that franchisors do better if they do not allow it. Passive ownership undermines the incentives that ownership provides to outlet operators to work hard. As Chapter 2, "The Advantages of Franchising," explained, one of the advantages that franchising provides to companies is that it uses the profit motive to motivate outlet operators to work hard and keep costs down. With passive ownership, the outlet operator becomes an employee again, with all of the incentive problems that such arrangements entail.

Sure, the passive-owner franchisee can come up with other incentives to get the employee running the outlet to work hard. However, whatever those incentives are, they will not be as effective as franchising. Equity ownership is the best mechanism for getting people to work hard, but providing equity is very difficult to do if the operator of the outlet is not the franchisee and the company is small and private, with illiquid stock. Furthermore, it will be hard for franchisees to figure out the right incentives to provide and the right controls to put in place if they have not actually run their outlets themselves. Many of the right incentives and controls can be learned only by operating the business and figuring out from that experience what the key dimensions are.

Passive ownership is also problematic because most passive owners do not put in sufficient time to develop their businesses. Because passive owners like to think of their businesses as investments, not jobs, they tend to treat them a bit like mutual funds. Rather than putting a lot of time and effort into figuring out the right way to satisfy customers or the right way to order raw materials, passive owners tend to let the businesses operate as they may, often with relatively poor performance.

Because of the problems that result from passive ownership, many successful franchisors do not allow it. For instance, Money Mailer, a direct-mail advertising franchisor out of Garden Grove, California, does not permit this ownership arrangement.[4] The requirement that owner-operators run their outlets has helped Money Mailer become one of the more successful direct-mail advertising franchisors.

Because passive ownership is problematic but multiunit franchising is desirable, some franchisors have sought hybrid solutions when they permit passive ownership. For instance, East Coast Original Frozen Custard, a frozen dessert franchisor out of Solon, Ohio, allows passive ownership but requires that the operator of the outlet own at least 15 percent of the stock in the franchisee company. The ownership requirement for the outlet operator mitigates some of the problems of passive ownership and helps make that arrangement more viable for franchisors.

Stop! Don't Do It!

1. Don't allow passive ownership in a new franchise system if you need to provide outlet operators with strong ownership incentives.

2. Don't reject passive ownership out of hand if the benefits from multiunit franchising are very high; the benefits might outweigh the costs.

Mechanisms to Control Franchisees

Another important category of policies that you need to get right to be a successful franchisor is the set of policies used to control franchisee behavior. The right policies include the following:

- Writing detailed contracts
- Reserving termination rights
- Controlling sources of supply
- Requiring exclusive dealing
- Ensuring payment of royalties
- Providing franchisees with excess profits

Writing Detailed Contracts

To be successful at franchising, you need to write contracts that carefully document the responsibilities and the commitments of your franchisees, as well as the consequences of failing to uphold these commitments. Careful contracting is essential to franchising because the system's brand name is a major asset of a franchised chain. Therefore, maintaining tight control over that brand name is very important to making sure that the system's goodwill is preserved.

Most successful franchisors are very careful to specify all the details of the quality standards that franchisees have to meet in their franchise agreements. For example, you cannot become a McDonald's franchisee until you agree to a contract that specifies how you will maintain cleanliness standards in your restaurant. The contract that you sign is quite specific: It tells how and when to clean the floors and the specific cleaning solution to use.

Similarly, the procedures and standards for producing the company's product or service are usually specified in great detail in the franchise agreement signed by the franchisor and franchisee. For example, many fast food franchisees specify minimum grades of meat and exact preparation times for products, to ensure that the final product meets the franchisor's standards.

Franchisees also have to agree to adhere to rules listed in usually fat operating manuals that outline a host of responsibilities, including maintaining the appearance of employee uniforms, preserving the format of company signs and storefronts, adhering to the service procedures for dealing with customers, sticking to acceptable uses of the trademark, adhering to standard operating procedures for the facility, making minimum advertising investments, and so on. For example, the typical franchise agreement requires franchisees to train employees according to franchisor protocols, and ensure that the employees provide proper standards of customer service and adhere to the franchisor's personal grooming and dress code. By specifying in detail the responsibilities and commitments of your franchisees, you'll find it easier for you to monitor them to make sure that they are doing what they are supposed to do.

The detailed controls specified in franchised contracts are not limited to franchisee behavior. They also include agreement to adhere to a standard outlet layout and to use only franchise system–authorized equipment. For instance, East Coast Original Frozen Custard requires that franchisee signs, cash registers, accounting systems, and equipment all meet franchisor specifications and be approved by the franchisor. It also requires franchisees to have any architectural drawings or construction documents for outlets approved in advance, as well as to decorate and equip the store according to standards set forth in the franchise agreement.

Many franchise agreements specify exactly what the franchisee needs to do to uphold the physical appearance of the franchise outlets. For instance, franchisors often require franchisees to repair or replace damaged signs, equipment, fixtures, and furnishing, and to repaint and replace wallpaper and upholstery in the outlets on a specified schedule.

Reserving Termination Rights

When you franchise, you'll also want spell out your rights to terminate the franchise agreement and take back the outlet if one of your franchisees fails to uphold system standards or fails to follow the policies and procedures as stated in your franchise agreement. Moreover, you will want to make sure that your franchise contract gives your franchisees the right to use your operating system, brand name, and trademarks *only* if they adhere to the rules of your system. You should make it a requirement that your franchisees return your operating manual upon expiration or termination of the franchise agreement. By reserving the right to terminate franchisees if they do not adhere to the rules and regulations of your franchise system, and to preclude them from using your procedures, brand name, and equipment if they are terminated, you increase the likelihood that your franchisees will play by the rules.

Termination of franchisees, however, is a complex legal process and one that is difficult to execute quickly in many states. We discuss the differences in state termination laws in greater detail in Chapter 10, "The Legal and Institutional Environment for Franchising." For now, suffice it to say that some states give franchisees many more opportunities than other states give them to cure problems that they have. Because state laws often weaken termination rights, many franchisors adopt policies that make it possible to sanction franchisees by taking actions well short of termination. At Tastee Freez, for example, the company sells franchisees the freezer necessary for making its frozen concoction but only leases the pump used to make Tastee Freez. This arrangement allows the company to terminate a franchisee's lease to the pump if he or she engages in problematic behavior.[5] Because the termination of the lease is easier and quicker to execute than the termination of the entire franchise agreement, this approach is effective at controlling franchisee behavior.

Controlling Sources of Supply

Another tool to control franchisee behavior that is available to you as a franchisor is limiting the sources of supply for raw materials. You can do this by specifying in your franchise agreement where franchisees can buy the supplies that they need. However, limiting sources of franchisee supply is a tricky game for franchisors to play. By law, you are permitted to require franchisees to purchase inputs from specified suppliers only if the inputs are proprietary to a system, such as with KFC's 11 herbs and spices. Sources of supply for generic inputs, such as plates or cups at a KFC, cannot be mandated. Therefore, if there is no relationship between the value of the trademarked name and the input, the franchisor cannot require the franchisee to use a particular source of supply.

This legal limitation makes it possible for the franchisee to select a source of supply that is not in keeping with the standards of the system. (For instance, the franchisee could choose paper cups that leak.) Therefore, franchisors often control input quality without violating franchise law sometimes by providing a list of approved suppliers and other times by specifying key product characteristics (for example, the thickness of the paper cups).[6]

Requiring Exclusive Dealing

Successful franchisors also preclude franchisees from selling the products of other companies, as a way to ensure the value of the brand name. For instance, McDonalds doesn't allow its franchisees to sell Pizza Hut pizza, and Coldwell Banker® does not allow its franchisees to rent furniture under the Aaron's Rent-to-Own brand. If your franchisees could sell other products or services, you would benefit less from the development of your brand name, and this would undermine your investment in developing that name. Therefore, you should specify in your franchise agreement that your franchisees are not allowed to sell products or services provided by other companies.

East Coast Original Frozen Custard's franchise agreement provides a good illustration of the exclusive dealing clause. This company requires its franchisees to sell only its custard and yogurt items in the form described on its standard menu. Any additional menu items offered by franchisees have to be approved by the franchisor before sale.

Most successful franchisors also give themselves the right to purchase any outlet that franchisees seek to sell, as well as to deny any sale to a franchisee that they see as unfit. They do this to ensure that the goodwill that accrues to the brand name belongs to them. By reserving the right of first refusal on sales, franchisors can also minimize the threat of opportunistic renegotiation of contracts by franchisees. This is important because there are costs to finding new franchisees for a given location. Therefore, you do not want franchisees to be able to threaten to leave the system to strike a better deal with you.

Of course, reserving the right of first refusal will raise your franchisees' fears that you will use this right to force them to strike a better deal with you through opportunistic renegotiation. To minimize this fear among your franchisees, you might want to couple the right of first refusal with a clause in the contract stating predetermined valuation in the event that the first refusal right is used.[7]

Ensuring Royalty Payments

As is discussed in greater detail in Chapter 8, "Pricing Franchises," most of your compensation as a franchisor is likely to come from royalties paid by your franchisees on gross sales of products or services made to end customers at their outlets. Because franchisee profits are earned net of these royalty payments, franchisees have a strong incentive to under-report the royalties that they owe you. Consequently, you need to establish effective mechanisms to ensure accurate payment of royalties on your franchisees' use of your system and trade name.

This can be accomplished in a variety of ways. First, you can employ mechanisms that make it harder for franchisees to under-report their sales. For example, East Coast Original Frozen Custard requires its franchisees to use specific electronic cash registers that cannot erase or reset sales, as a way to provide the franchisor with accurate sales information.

You can also audit franchisees and punish them for inaccurate reporting. For example, many franchisors reserve the right to audit franchisee sales records at will, imposing the cost of the audit on the franchisee if they find under-reporting of sales by more than 2 percent. In addition, franchisors tend to impose punitive penalties on franchisees that are caught under-reporting, or they make under-reporting of sales grounds for terminating the franchise agreement.

Providing Franchisees with Excess Profits

Another way to control franchisee behavior is to provide franchisees with an excess profit stream that makes them want to stay in the franchise system. Making franchises so profitable for franchisees that they have no reason to cheat is a very effective approach. It minimizes the need for franchisors to figure out what franchises are doing to ensure that franchisees play by the rules.

Providing excess profits to franchisees as a way to ensure that franchisees play by the rules of the franchise system is surprisingly common. One study examined 45 franchise systems and found that the average net present value of excess profits provided to franchisees over the life of a franchise agreement was $382,495. For McDonald's, a very desirable system to be in, the net present value of these excess profits exceeded $1 million.[8] With excess profits like these, it is not surprising that relatively few franchisees cheat and risk losing this lucrative arrangement.

Stop! Don't Do It!

1. Don't forget to write detailed contracts to control the behavior of your franchisees.
2. Don't extract all of the profits of your system from franchisees; it will make controlling them much more difficult.

Term of the Contract

As a franchisor, you will need to set the term of your franchise agreement and the term of any renewal periods that you offer to your franchisees. A very small number of franchisors offer contracts in perpetuity, and another small handful offer contracts with no time length at all. The vast majority of franchisors offer some fixed time period for the contract, and 91 percent offer franchisees the right to renew their contracts upon expiration. The average term of a franchise contract is ten years, with an eight-year renewal.

However, this term varies substantially by industry. The printing and copying industry offers contracts that average almost 19 years, with 18-year renewals; the travel industry, on the other hand, offers contracts that average only 6 years, with 5-year renewals.[9] Even the right to renew varies across industries. The majority of franchisors in a variety of industries offer the right to renew, but only a third of lodging franchisors offer this right.[10] Table 5.1 provides some data on average contract length for several industries.

TABLE 5.1 Average Contract Length for Selected Industries

Industry	Contract Length in Years
Printing and copying	18.6
Lodging	15.4
Restaurants	13.8
Fast food	12.2
Baked goods	11.4
Sports and recreation	11.3
Auto repair	11.2
Retail	10.1
Child related	9.4
Maintenance	9.3
Services	9.1
Retail food	8.8
Personnel services	8.7
Building and construction	8.3
Business services	7.5
Real estate	7.3
Education	7.2
Travel	5.7
Overall	**10.3**

Source: Adapted from data contained in IFA Educational Foundation's *The Profile of Franchising* (Washington, DC: IFA, 1998).

Although industry is an important source of variation in contract term, the franchise contract term varies substantially within industries. Take, for example, the commercial office cleaning business. Janetize America, a franchisor from Livonia, Michigan, offers 10-year contracts with a 10-year renewal period; whereas its competitor, Jani-King® International, out of Addison, Texas, offers 20-year contracts with a 20-year renewal period.[11] This variation within the industry means that you need to think about what your strategy is as a franchisor to determine the right term for your franchise contracts.

Setting the right contract term is important for you, as a franchisor, because your franchisees will not invest in developing a customer base in their local market (and other forms of goodwill) unless they can capture the returns to that investment. The longer the term of your franchise agreement is, the greater is the time period over which your franchisees can amortize their investments, so the more willing they will be to make a large investment. Take, for example, getting your franchisees to invest in the proprietary design for your building, the golden gates. The franchisees will have to give up the use of this proprietary design if they are no longer in your franchise system. Therefore, your franchisees will want a long enough contract to make sure that they can generate a reasonable return on their investment in creating the golden gates.

Moreover, a long-term contract facilitates the ability of a franchisee to sell his or her business. The value of a business depends in part on the future stream of earnings that the business will create. If the future contract time horizon isn't very long when the franchisee seeks to sell the business, its value is decreased. Thus, having a long-term contract makes franchising more attractive to franchisees by making their businesses more valuable if they seek to sell them.

Having a long-term contract is also important because it will make it harder for you, as a franchisor, to threaten not to renew your franchisees as a way to opportunistically extract some of the franchisee's profit. Historically, a not-too-small number of franchisors have given franchising a bad name by making their franchise contracts short and renewal difficult as a way of opportunistically extracting a better deal from franchisees. By threatening not to renew a franchisee, a franchisor can get the franchisee to accept terms that transfer additional amounts of franchisee profit to the franchisor, such as higher royalty rates.

Although I am not saying that you would do this (it is not the most ethical practice), you need to be aware that some people engage in this activity. As a result, many franchisees are wary of this occurring and do not like to sign short-term contracts for franchises.

Long-term contracts also give your franchisees an incentive to adhere to the rules of the franchise system. As long as participation in the franchise system is profitable to your franchisees, the longer the period of time that remains on the franchise contract, the greater the amount of future profit the franchises will have to give up if they are caught doing something wrong. This potential for the loss of future profits will lower your franchisees' willingness to cheat. After all, when they can earn the very high profits of being a McDonald's franchisee for another decade, they probably will be unwilling to risk those profits by cheating on the quality of their hamburger buns.

The importance of long-term contracts in deterring cheating and ensuring that franchisees adhere to the rules of the system increases as the franchise system gets larger. The more outlets there are in a chain, the more locations display the brand, increasing its value and creating an incentive for franchisees to free-ride by under-investing in advertising. Moreover, because there are economies of scale in advertising, franchisors advertise their brand names more heavily as they grow, further increasing the potential benefits of franchisee free riding. Therefore, as the franchise system gets larger, long-term contracts become more important as a way to provide franchisees with enough of a future profit stream to deter cheating.

Of course, offering long-term contracts to your franchisees is not without its own problems. If you offer your franchisees short-term contracts, it can be easier for you to change your system than if you offer them long-term agreements. Take, for example, your royalty rate. If you have 20-year contracts and you charge a royalty that is too low for you to make a profit, it will be a long time before you can correct this problem. You will have to wait for your initial agreements to expire to get your royalty rate up to a profitable level. And there is a good chance that you won't last long enough as a franchisor to make this correction. However, if your contracts are only three years, you can probably correct the problem of having too low of a royalty rate before it dooms your franchise.

Having long-term contracts also will be a problem if you aren't very good at picking your franchisees. As was said earlier, it is a lot easier not to renew a franchisee than it is to terminate a franchisee for poor performance. So, if you are picking losers as your franchisees, you can get saddled with the wrong people for a long time with long-term agreements. You can mitigate this problem with short-term agreements and learn which franchisees to select by the time you make the second round of franchisee selection.

Finally, having long-term contracts can lead your outlets to look dated and stale. In general, franchise agreements call for upgrading only at renewal time. For example, East Coast Original Frozen Custard requires its franchisees to completely refurbish and remodel the signage, equipment, decor, and interiors in their outlets at the time of renewal, but it requires maintenance only prior to the renewal point.

If your business is one in which decor changes often, your outlets can start to look pretty dated if your system has long-term contracts. You've probably seen this as you've traveled around the country. Some older franchise outlets in longer established chains, such as Dairy Queen®, look like something out of a 1980s movie.

Stop! Don't Do It!

1. Don't sign short-term contracts with franchisees if you want them to invest heavily in system-specific assets.

2. Don't sign long-term contracts with franchisees if you are unsure of the right policies or procedures, royalty rates, or fees for your franchise; you are unlikely to last until you can fix those policies if you have gotten them wrong.

Franchisee Advertising

Advertising is an important part of most franchised businesses. As was explained in earlier chapters, brand names are an important asset for attracting end customers to franchised outlets, and advertising is a crucial tool to building brand names. Therefore, it is hardly surprising that policies toward franchisee investment in advertising are important ones for you, as a franchisor, to get right when you establish your system. These policies can be divided into two categories: those focused on national advertising funds and those geared toward local advertising.

National Advertising

To be successful, you need to build the brand name reputation of your franchise system. Most of the ideas underlying new franchise systems can be copied relatively easily by other firms, making your brand name a very important source of competitive advantage. In fact, research shows that new franchisors who have built up their brand names successfully over time are more likely to survive than those who have not developed their brand names.[12]

Moreover, brand names are valuable because they help to attract new customers in new markets. A chain business often attracts customers in a new location because the customers know the firm's quality from its brand name reputation even before they have encountered it. For example, many people know that Wal-Mart® offers good quality at low prices even in locations where Wal-Mart has yet to establish a store. The benefits of brand names to franchise systems means that you need to advertise your franchise's product or service to build its brand name when you begin franchising.

Franchisors generally fund the advertising that they use to build their brand names by establishing a fund to which franchisees are required by contract to contribute, and this is used to pay for national advertising. For example, Mister Money, a pawn loan and check-cashing franchise, charges a 3 percent advertising fee.[13] This means that its franchisees pay 3 percent of their gross revenues into a fund managed by the franchisor to pay for national advertising.

Statistics from the International Franchise Association show that approximately 72 percent of all franchisors have a national advertising fund. However, the use of national advertising funds varies by industry: Only 48 percent of business service franchises have such funds, but 88 percent of restaurants use them.[14] Of course, one reason for this variation is that some industries, such as restaurants, rely more heavily on advertising to bring in customers than other industries, such as business services, which are more reliant on word-of-mouth. Table 5.2 provides the percentage of franchisors with national advertising fees for selected industries.

TABLE 5.2 Percentage of Franchisors with a National Advertising Fee, by Industry

Industry	Percentage of Franchisors with Ad Fee
Lodging	78
Fast food	72
Restaurants	70
Baked goods	59
Child related	55
Real estate	50
Sports and recreation	48
Education related	47
Retail food	46
Personnel services	45
Printing and copying	44
Maintenance services	43
Retail	43
Building and construction	41
Auto repair	39
Services	39
Business services	30
Travel agencies	9
Overall	**52**

Source: Adapted from data contained in the IFA Educational Foundation's *The Profile of Franchising* (Washington, DC: IFA, 1998).

To be successful as a franchisor in most industries, you need to *require* your franchisees to pay a percentage of their revenues into a common advertising pool that you manage. Why? Without advertising, you will be unable to build your system brand name. Economies of scale in advertising mean that you want to have all of the outlets in your system pool their advertising dollars rather than invest individually. And franchisees won't advertise collectively unless you require it of them. Remember from Chapter 3, "The Disadvantages of Franchising," that franchisees have an incentive to free-ride if they can benefit from advertising in a particular media market but not pay for it. Franchisees can get additional customers at no cost by free riding off the efforts of others to pay for advertising in a given media market. You can mitigate this free riding problem by specifying an advertising fee in your franchise agreement. Because your franchisees will be required to pay a percentage of their gross sales for advertising, which you invest, they cannot free-ride as easily as if you do not require them to invest.

Although there is some variance in how national advertising fees are set up, the majority of franchisors (52 percent) set up national advertising fees as a percentage of gross revenues on franchisee sales; only 5 percent charge franchisees a flat rate. Why is there variance in how national advertising is set up? Some part of the difference in the structure of advertising fees is a function of industry. For example, 78 percent of lodging franchisors use a percentage approach, while 36 percent of travel agencies use a flat fee.[15] This difference results from the nature of how sales are earned in an industry, making it easier to use flat rates in industry such as travel agencies than in industries such as lodging.

However, even within industries, some companies adopt flat rate advertising fees and others set up advertising as a percentage of sales. For instance, Jackson Hewitt® Tax Service, a tax-preparation franchise out of Parsippany, New Jersey, charges franchisees a national advertising fee of 6 percent of gross sales; whereas its competitor,

Liberty® Tax Service, out of Virginia Beach, Virginia, charges franchisees a flat rate of between $6,000 and $7,000 per year.

The differences in how advertising fees are assessed result from different strategies for how franchisors want to manage their businesses. If you use a percentage rate, your largest franchisees will pay a higher portion of your advertising budget. Consequently, if there is a declining return to scale in advertising, your largest franchisees will get the lowest per-dollar return on their investment in the fund and are likely to grumble about this arrangement. In contrast, if there is an increasing return to scale to advertising, having a flat fee will benefit your largest franchisees more than your smallest ones, leading the latter to be the complainers. Thus, depending on the nature of returns to scale in advertising in your industry, you might want to go with flat fees instead of a percentage of gross sales as a way to set up your national advertising fund.

Legally, national advertising funds need to be treated as trust funds and kept separate from royalty payments to franchisors. That is, the franchisor can use these funds to pay only for advertising. Acceptable types of activities paid for by advertising funds include newspaper inserts, direct-mail flyers, point-of-sale promotional items, and radio and television advertisements. They are not supposed to be used for other purposes of the franchise. For instance, franchisors cannot use these funds to pay for expenses associated with selling franchises or as a source of funds to overcome temporary cash-flow crises.[16]

One important point for you to consider when you set up your franchise system is that national advertising is rarely used when franchise systems are young, but it tends to be adopted as franchisors grow and expand across the country. After all, there really is little reason to conduct national advertising when you operate only five outlets, all in the Louisville, Kentucky, metro area. Because you probably aren't going to engage in national advertising when you first get started franchising, you might to write a fee for national advertising into your franchise agreement but not require franchisees to pay into the national advertising fund until your franchise system has reached sufficient size for you to undertake national advertising. By setting up a national advertising fee and specifying when you are going to start using it, you make it possible to start national advertising without having to go through the costly and difficult process of renegotiating your franchise agreements. At the same time, you can make your franchise system more attractive to potential franchisees by making the cost of operating an outlet cheaper for them than participation in a national chain. By not collecting several percentage points of gross revenue as an advertising fee initially, your franchisees can save money on their royalty payments.

For example, Lox of Bagels, a Potomac, Maryland, retail bagel bakery with only 13 franchisors, does not charge a national advertising fee.[17] With 13 franchisees located in only a few geographic locations, this company cannot yet engage in national advertising. The company's decision not to charge a national advertising fee helps it attract franchisees because most other bagel franchises charge a national advertising fee of several percent of gross sales.

Some franchisors require their franchisees to pay into the national advertising fund from day one of the franchise system because they conduct some national advertising even when they are very small. However, the level of that advertising is small compared to what they plan to conduct once they have grown larger. Therefore, their agreements with franchisees call for a small national advertising fee initially, but increase the amount of this payment when the franchise system reaches a certain size. For instance, East Coast Original Frozen Custard's franchise agreement calls for advertising fund payments made by franchisees to increase by 1 percent when the franchise system has 15 outlets in it.

Local Advertising

Because most new franchisors start small and are geographically limited in their operations at first, national advertising is not the major tool that they use to attract customers and build their brand name—at least, not initially. Instead, local advertising efforts are more important.

Franchisors typically manage local advertising by requiring franchisees to make an investment of a set percentage of sales for the local promotion of the store. East Coast Original Frozen Custard, for instance, requires its franchisees to invest 1 percent of sales in local advertising, including the cost of all promotional materials, advertising, and prizes and promotions. This requirement ensures that franchisees advertise their businesses but does not call for any national pooling of that advertising effort.

Some augmenting of local advertising funds, however, is often advantageous in franchising. Therefore, for local advertising, many franchisors engage in cooperative advertising. Cooperative advertising is an agreement between a franchisor and a franchisee to share the cost of advertising. For example, ServiceMaster Clean®, a franchisor of cleaning services out of Memphis, Tennessee, has cooperative advertising arrangements in which it and its franchisees jointly pay for local ads.[18]

Roughly one-third of all advertising undertaken by franchisors is done through cooperative advertising, and roughly one-third of all franchisors engage in cooperative advertising. Among new and small franchisors, and or more regionally oriented franchise systems that do not see the value in national advertising, cooperative advertising is more common.[19] Cooperative advertising is also common when the effect of advertising on customer demand tends to spill over outside the franchisee's geographic area, making the likelihood of free riding high. Under these circumstances, you, as a franchisor, want to use additional incentives to make sure that your franchisees invest in advertising. Cooperative advertising is an effective tool to do just that.

Stop! Don't Do It!

1. Don't fail to require your franchisees to make contributions to national advertising funds.

2. Don't forget to use local advertising to build your brand name when your system is new and small and national advertising is not yet economical.

Complements

Although this chapter has discussed individually the different policies that you need to be a successful franchisor, this was done largely for expositional purposes. In actuality, you want to consider your franchise policies as bundles of complementary policies. Complementary policies are policies that work best when they are adopted jointly rather than when one policy is adopted alone. For example, this chapter discussed the value of both long-term contracts and the value of franchisee termination clauses. Both of these policies are important independently for the reasons outlined earlier, but they are actually complementary, making them particularly valuable when adopted jointly. Long-term contracts are very helpful because they encourage franchisee compliance with the rules of the franchise system and because they reduce franchisee fears of opportunistic franchisor nonrenewal of contracts. But these benefits come at a cost: Franchisee termination is more difficult than nonrenewal of franchisee contracts. Therefore, when your franchise contracts are long term, you are much better off if you ensure that you have the right provisions to terminate franchisees without excessive cost or difficulty.[20] Figure 5.1 illustrates the complementary relationship between long-term contracts and termination provisions.

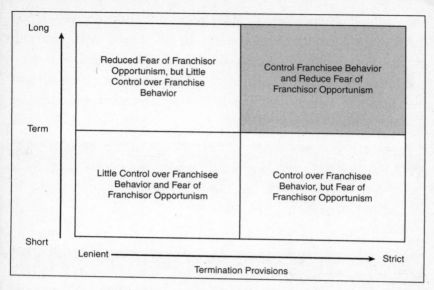

Figure 5.1 The Complementary Relationship Between Long-Term Contracts and Strict Termination Provisions

The relationship between contract term and strictness of termination provisions is only one example of complementary relationships between policies. There are many others. The example is provided not to be comprehensive, but to illustrate the importance of developing your franchise system's policies as a system rather than in piecemeal fashion. You are better off figuring out the best combination of policies (even if each of the policies alone seems like it might not be the best one) than you are figuring out the best policy in each category—say, the best contract length and the best termination provisions—but having these policies be inconsistent with each other.

Of course, the value of complementary relationships between policies in franchising makes developing the right policies for your franchise system a whole lot harder. If the right approach is just to pick the best individual policies, benchmarking the best existing franchise systems is pretty easy. You can ask around, and soon you will know who has the right approach to contract length, advertising policies, or termination provisions. However, when policies are complementary and you have to adopt the right combinations to be successful, this benchmarking strategy doesn't work very well. If you do it, you will end up with a hodgepodge of, at best, inefficient and, at worst, contradictory policies. What you really need to do is get a good franchise advisor who understands the underlying economics of franchising to help you design a system that takes advantage of complementary policies.

Stop! Don't Do It!

1. Don't adopt your system policies in piecemeal fashion; adopt complementary policies together.

Questions to Ask Yourself

1. Should I require my franchisees to operate their own outlets?

2. What provisions should I include in my franchise contracts to control the behavior of my franchisees?

3. How will I verify the compliance of franchisees with the rules and policies of the franchise system?

4. How many years should by franchise contract be? And should I permit renewal? If so, how long should renewal be?

5. What type of advertising (amount and form) do I need to increase demand among end customers?

6. Which of my policies reinforce and enhance others? Which policies should I adopt together?

Summary

This chapter identified four areas in which it is important to adopt the right policies if you want to be successful at franchising: rules toward ownership of franchised outlets; mechanisms to ensure that franchisees act in the best interest of the franchise system; policies establishing the right term for a franchise agreement, as well as its possible renewal; and mechanisms to ensure franchisee advertising of the system brand name, both national and local.

As a franchisor, you can require your franchisees to operate their outlets directly or allow them to be passive owners. Allowing passive ownership is more common than requiring owner operation, but it is not a very effective approach to franchising. Passive ownership undermines the basic incentives of franchising for the outlet operator. Consequently, passive ownership tends to be a good idea only when it is used as a way to allow talented franchisees to operate multiple units simultaneously.

To be successful as a franchisor, you need to write agreements with your franchisees that control their behavior. Successful franchisors write contracts that carefully document the responsibilities and commitments of franchisees, as well as the consequences to franchisees (usually termination of the agreement) of failing to uphold these commitments. Because termination is costly and difficult, successful franchisors also employ other tools to control franchisee behavior, such as specifying sources of supply. Although dictating specific suppliers is fine for proprietary inputs, antitrust laws preclude you, as a franchisor, from dictating suppliers for generic inputs. For generic inputs, you need to provide your franchisees with a list of approved suppliers, as a way to control their behavior.

Another way to control franchisee behavior is to put exclusive dealing clauses in your franchise contracts, limiting your franchisees to selling only your brand of products or services. This ensures that the franchisee's investment in building the outlet's goodwill goes to your brand. Finally, as a franchisor, you can control your franchisees' behavior by providing them with excess profit that serves as an incentive to conform, lest they lose that valuable profit stream through termination.

A third important issue for you to consider is the term of your franchise contract. Although both industry and firm strategy influence the right length for a contract, the decision essentially comes down to a balancing act: You must balance the importance of encouraging franchisees to invest in the development of the outlet's goodwill on the one hand with your need to modify the system on the other.

A final area in which you, as a franchisor, need to develop the right policies is advertising, which is central to the development of your system's brand name. You must require franchisees to invest in a national advertising fund, or you will face under-investment in your brand name from franchisee free riding. In the early years of your system, you will probably want to have a national advertising fund on the books but exempt franchisees from investing in it. In addition, while your system is primarily local, you will want to use cooperative ads to support local advertising.

Now that you understand the right policies for successful franchising, we turn to a discussion of the right support services to offer your franchisees. This is the subject of the next chapter.

6

FRANCHISEE SUPPORT AND ASSISTANCE

Figuring out the right type and amount of support to offer franchises will enhance the performance of your franchise system. If you provide the wrong type of support, or not enough of it, your system will do poorly because you will not provide potential franchisees with the things that will attract them to the system, nor will you give people the assistance that they need if they become franchisees. On the other hand, if you provide your franchisees with too much support, even if it is the right type of support, you will end up attracting people without the entrepreneurial skills that you want to make your business a success. Moreover, you will saddle yourself with costs that will undermine your margins as a franchisor or, worse yet, drive potential franchisees to your competitors by charging them high fees to recoup those costs.

In general, you need to get four categories of support right in your franchise system:

- The training that you provide franchisees to get them ready to operate an outlet in your system

- Ongoing support services, such as centralized data processing and inventory control or communications mechanisms, that you offer to franchisees

- Real estate services (for the vast majority of franchise systems that have physical locations) that you offer franchisees to help them to identify the right locations for their businesses

- The assistance that you provide franchisees in obtaining financing for their businesses

To be successful at franchising, you need to figure out the right types and amounts of these four categories of services and determine who should pay for them. This chapter offers specific information to help you assess the right type and level of support to provide franchisees in these four areas.

Training

As a franchisor, you are selling a system for operating your business to your franchisees. To make use of this system and operate an outlet of your business successfully, your franchisees need some type of initial training. Although you are never going to be able to train your franchisees in everything that you have learned about outlet operations from operating your company-owned stores, you do need to give them enough knowledge to run the business without you being present.

Giving your franchisees this level of understanding means training them in all of the key areas of your business before they begin running their outlets. For instance, the founders of East Coast

Custard, a franchisor out of Solon, Ohio, seek to provide franchisees "with instruction and hands on training in every fact of an operation…diligently developed of the last 18 years…[including] production and quality control, equipment maintenance, advertising and promotion methods, and other operation techniques"[1] before they open their outlets. In addition, before they get started, you need to give your franchisees some sense of where to look for answers to problems that occur in the operation of their businesses, whether that is from you directly or in the operating manuals that you provide to them.

Research suggests that this means providing your franchisees with adequate preopening training. Franchisors that provide their franchisees with more than the average level of training in an industry are more likely to survive over time. Why? Training helps franchisees perform as outlet operators, which boosts sales and returns for the franchisor. It also helps attract franchisees at a lower cost. Many franchisees choose to buy a franchise because they lack expertise in an industry. As a result, they use the level of training that they will receive as a selection criterion in choosing among franchises. If you offer better training than other franchisors, you will find franchisees easier to attract than if your training is perceived as inadequate or even limited.

However, this doesn't mean that you should just offer your franchisees endless amounts of training. The benefits of the training that you offer are offset by the costs of providing that training. Whether you charge franchisees directly for the cost of training or build that cost into your franchise fee, your franchisees will incur a cost for obtaining training that will affect their returns from buying your franchise. Because the marginal benefits of training decline with the amount of training that you provide (200 hours of training is not likely to make you twice as good a house-cleaning franchisee as 100 hours of training), but the costs of training tend increase in a linear manner with the number of hours of training, there is generally an optimal amount of training that you need to provide to your franchisees. Whether that optimal amount is a few days or a few months depends on the nature of your industry, the complexity of your product, the learning curve for your business, and a host of other things. To figure out how much training to provide your franchisees, you need to quantify the costs and benefits of training and determine how much both of these change with the amount of training provided. This calculation will allow you to figure out the optimal amount of training to provide to your franchisees.

In addition to figuring out how much training to provide, you need to figure out where to provide it. Some of your franchisee training might be offered at your headquarters, while other training might occur at the franchisee's location. For instance, the Norfolk, Virginia, computer assistance franchise Geeks on Call® provides four days of training at the company's headquarters and one to three days in the franchisee's territory. In contrast, RadioShack® Select, a franchisor of consumer electronics stores out of Fort Worth, Texas, provides five days of on-site training to its franchisees, but no training at the franchisor's headquarters.[2]

Your choice of where to provide training depends, again, on the nature of your business and your industry. Some types of business operations in some industries are hard to teach in the absence of "learning by doing." For example, an ice cream business isn't really learned very easily without making and selling ice cream. These types of franchises have a chunk of their training at franchisees' locations. Other types of businesses can be learned relatively well from books but require information on the centralized operations of the firm. An example of this type of business might be a retail computer store. This category of franchises will provide most of its training at the franchisor's headquarters.

Often franchisors will provide initial store opening assistance to their franchisees. This assistance consists of placing a franchisee field consultant at the franchisee's location for the first days of the franchisee's operation to help the franchisee with problem solving in overcoming the issues and obstacles faced in first operating the franchise outlet. For instance, The Crack Team®, a franchisor of foundation wall-repair services, out of St. Louis, Missouri, provides assistance to franchisees at their opening. Similarly, East Coast Custard provides a field operations representative for the first five days of a store's operations. Because of the complexity of the initial opening and setup of an operation, many franchisees find this type of assistance and training to be quite valuable.

Not all franchisee training occurs prior to the establishment of the franchise system, however. Some franchisors provide additional field training to their franchisees after the franchisee's operation has become established. One reason for later field training is that franchisees are more likely to remember and use the training that they receive if they get some of it after they have started their businesses rather than receiving all of it before opening their outlets.

Another reason that franchisors provide field training after the franchisees have begun operations is to introduce new products or services that require some franchisee training. Not only does the field training help franchisees to provide the new products and services to end customers, but also it is very useful for selling franchisees on new products or processes. As Chapter 3, "The Disadvantages of Franchising," explained, because franchisees are independent businesspeople, you cannot command them to adopt innovations. Rather, you must persuade them to do so. Without field training, you are likely to find it quite difficult to persuade your franchisees to go along with innovations that you have developed.

The benefit of field training is greatest for franchisors that offer new products or services to franchisees that require assistance to understand but are not available when the franchisor first set up the system. For instance, a bakery franchise that expanded into selling coffee might benefit from field training because it provides a way for franchisees to get the training that they need in the provision of the new product without leaving their outlets.

Field training can be provided either as part of the franchise fee paid to the franchisor or at an extra charge. For instance, Valpak® Direct Marketing, a franchisor of cooperative mailings out of Largo, Florida, provides field training as part of its franchise fee.[3] Other franchisees, however, charge extra for this field training as a way to keep costs down for franchisees that do not use it.

Field training can also be in person or by telephone. For example, East Coast Custard makes field representatives available at franchisee locations periodically, but makes those representatives available by telephone at other times. Most franchisees find greater value in field training that is offered in person because of the greater assistance that can be provided if the franchise field consultant is present at the franchisee's location. However, in-person assistance greatly increases the cost of field training and, in many cases, makes that form of training too costly to be worthwhile.

Whether you should provide field training to your franchisees depends a lot on the size of your franchise system. Research shows that new franchisors that offer lesser amounts of field support to their franchisees are more likely to survive over time.[4] This is because in-person field training can be very costly to provide unless a system has a large number of franchised outlets that are clustered geographically. Most new franchise systems do not have large numbers of franchised outlets clustered in narrow geographic areas, leading the cost, in terms of time and money, of traveling between locations to quickly offset the benefits of field training.

However, as franchisors grow larger, they tend to perform better if they provide more field training. Field training offers an important mechanism to control the franchisee free riding problem, which grows with system size. By providing additional training, you, the franchisor, get another chance to check on the operations of your franchisee. You also can build a stronger relationship between your operation and that of your franchisees, which makes them think twice about breaking system rules. In addition, as your system grows, you can achieve more economies of scale in field training, making its provision much more economical than when you first begin franchising.

Stop! Don't Do It!

1. Don't franchise without developing a plan for training franchisees that includes the amount, form, and timing of the training.

2. Don't fail to examine the costs and benefits of training to figure out the optimal amount of training to provide to your franchisees.

Support Services

When you begin franchising, you also need to figure out what kinds of support services to provide to your franchisees as part of your system's operational strategy. In general, support services can be divided into three subcategories: field evaluation and consulting, centralized services, and communications.

Field Operations Evaluation

Field operations evaluation is the use of franchisor personnel to monitor the operations of franchisees by conducting field audits. Field operations evaluation is a key tool for making sure that franchisees adhere to the rules of the franchise system. Field audits provide an early warning system to identify the need for corrective action when franchisees deviate from system rules. They are particularly important in franchise operations, given the limited amount of real-time data that franchisors can gather from their franchised outlets. Therefore, many franchisors have field operations evaluation as part of their systems.

However, field operations evaluation is much like field training, in that it is quite costly for young franchise systems. This means that you might not want to provide field operations evaluation when you first establish your franchise system. The lack of scale economies in your operations can often lead the costs of field operations evaluation to outweigh the benefits. Although this is less likely to occur with field operations evaluation than with field training, you do need to evaluate the costs and benefits of field operations evaluation carefully in the earliest years of your franchise system. You might decide that the cost of field audits is too high to conduct them regularly when you first begin to franchise. For instance, East Coast Original Frozen Custard, a young franchisor with very few outlets, does not commit to regular field audits of its franchisees because of the cost of conducting those audits.

Centralized Services

A second category of franchisee services are what I call centralized services—things such as centralized data processing, central purchasing, and inventory control. These activities, along with efforts to build the system brand name, are the major sources of franchisor value added after the initial training of franchisees has been completed. Centralized services are important to provide to franchisees because they benefit significantly from economies of scale and learning curves. Concentrating these activities in the hands of franchisors reduces the costs of these activities, providing franchisees with savings relative to what they would achieve as independent businesspeople, and making participation in the franchise system financially attractive.

Of course, because centralized services are subject to scale economies, they provide increasing benefits as systems grow in size. Because the provision of centralized services enhances performance more for large systems, many systems do not provide these services when they are very small, but begin to provide them when they reach a large enough size for real cost savings to be achieved from their centralization. For instance, Express Oil Change, an auto service franchise out of Birmingham, Alabama, with 143 outlets, is now of a size that the provision of centralized data processing, central purchasing, and inventory control services for its franchisees is cost effective.[5]

Communication

A third area in which you need to develop effective policies toward franchisee support is the area of communications. Franchisors can use several tools to keep in touch with their franchisees and to help franchisees keep in touch with each other: toll-free telephone numbers, regional and national meetings, and newsletters. Toll-free telephone numbers are a useful support tool because they provide a way for franchisees to get information from headquarters when franchise consultants are not visiting them. Newsletters are a useful mechanism for transmitting information to franchisees about activities in other parts of the franchise system, as well as to provide information about franchisor developments. Regional and national meetings are helpful because they provide franchisees with a way to meet and exchange ideas, as well as to reinforce the common goals of the system.

Although these support services are valuable, they come at a cost that sometimes exceeds the benefits. They are most often used after franchise systems have grown large, rather than when the systems are first started and are small, because these communication support services provide greater performance benefits to larger franchise systems. By facilitating greater communication between franchisors and franchisees, these tools help to minimize the franchisee free riding problem, which grows with system size. In addition, franchisors can achieve economies of scale in communication as the system grows in size, making communication mechanisms much more cost effective after a franchisor has reached a certain scale.

How Many Services to Provide—and When to Start Offering Them

Another dimension of developing your approach to franchisee support services is deciding how many services you will have and how much of them to provide. This is tricky to do, particularly when your franchise system is young and small. The research evidence suggests that having an efficient headquarters operation is crucial to the performance of a new franchisor. For instance, one of my studies showed that the typical successful new franchisor operates seven outlets for every headquarters staff member, whereas the typical failed franchisor establishes only one outlet for every headquarters staff member.[6]

Having an efficient headquarters operation generally means providing limited support services to franchisees initially. So if offering additional services means hiring additional headquarters personnel and hindering your franchising span of control, you probably want to think about trimming your support services.

> ### Stop! Don't Do It!
>
> 1. Don't forget to use field operations evaluation, centralized services, and communications services, to provide value to your franchisees, particularly as your system grows in size.
> 2. Don't provide too many support services when your system is young; new franchisors do poorly if they have a low ratio of outlets to headquarters employees.

Real Estate Services

Many franchise systems operate in industries where physical locations are important. In these industries, success is often about location, location, location. This makes selecting the correct sites for outlets and negotiating real estate leases important to ensuring franchisee performance. Therefore, to be successful at franchising, you need to make sure that your franchisees manage site selection and lease negotiations effectively.

Site-Selection Assistance

One way that franchisors help their franchisees is by providing them with assistance with selecting the right sites. For instance, Physicians Weight Loss Centers® of America, a franchisor of weight-reduction services, offers site-selection assistance to its franchisees.[7] Site-selection assistance can include a variety of forms of help from traffic pattern studies, to preselection of promising locations, to a variety of other things. However, whatever specific form site-selection assistance takes, it involves transferring franchisor knowledge of what makes a good location to franchisees.

Site-selection assistance is a valuable service for you to provide to your franchisees for several reasons. Historically, the best-performing franchises have owned the real estate on which their franchise outlets sit and have leased those locations to franchisees. The value of real estate to system performance means that picking the right locations is a valuable capability for a franchisor to develop and, once it is developed, can provide a useful service to offer to franchisees. If franchisors have experience at site selection, they can often make more accurate site-selection decisions than the average franchisee, enhancing the performance of the entire system when site-selection assistance is provided.

Providing site selection to your franchisees is also a good idea because it provides you with a mechanism to manage the flow of financial returns from your franchise system. As was discussed in Chapter 3, franchisors and franchisees disagree about the optimal locations for the establishment of additional franchised outlets. If you select the locations for your franchisee's outlets, you can add outlets in places that maximize the financial returns to you of increasing the size of your system. However, if your franchisees conduct site selection, you cannot ensure that the additional outlets will be established in the best locations for you.

When you first start your franchise, the advantages of providing site selection support just described might be outweighed by the value of local real estate knowledge provided by your franchisees. Because you have little knowledge of the real estate market where you are establishing your first outlets and need to rely on your franchisees to provide that information to you, you might not want to provide site-selection assistance when you first establish your franchise system. Instead, when you first start out, you likely will be more successful if you delegate local market real estate activities to your franchisees and focus on building your system's assets and brand name.[8] By transferring the tasks of identifying locations to franchisees with local market knowledge, you can grow your system more rapidly.

However, as your system grows in size, the value of providing site-selection assistance increases. The probability that your franchisees will have unique local market knowledge decreases with the number of times you have franchised because most locations have something in common with other locations. As a result, franchisee real estate knowledge becomes less of something that you need to obtain as your system becomes larger. Moreover, your ability to specify the exact locations of franchised outlets increases with the number of outlets in the system, making site-selection assistance more important for large systems than for small ones. Consequently, as your system becomes larger, you want to develop site-selection assistance and offer it to your franchisees.

Lease-Negotiation Assistance

Another form of real estate assistance that you can offer to your franchisees is lease-negotiation assistance, which is help with navigating the issues of establishing lease agreements (things such as understanding tenant improvements and percentage rents).[9] Many franchisors offer this assistance to their franchisees. Fantastic Sams®, a hair care franchise out of Anaheim, California, is one example.[10]

As with site-selection assistance, you might want to delegate lease negotiation to franchisees when you first start your system. Besides relying initially on the local market knowledge that franchisees have, you might want to do this as a way to ensure that your first franchisees invest in system-specific assets (such as a unique building layout). You will find this much easier to accomplish if you let your franchisees control the terms of the leasehold. When your franchisees have more control of their leaseholds, they are less likely to worry that you will opportunistically take advantage of your control over the lease to strike a better deal with them.

As your system becomes more established, you will (hopefully) develop a reputation for fair dealing, which will mitigate this fear of opportunism among your franchisees and potential franchisees. Thus, letting them control the terms of the leasehold won't be as important in reassuring them that you will treat them right as it was when you first got started. When the franchisees' fears that you will engage in opportunistic behavior are no longer so dominant, you are better off controlling the leases to your franchisees' locations because subleasing real estate to your franchisees is an effective way to generate additional income from your system. For example, by buying or leasing real estate that is then subleased to franchisees at a set markup, McDonald's has created a strong revenue stream for itself that is both independent of the revenue stream from franchising the rights to sell McDonald's hamburgers and more lucrative.

You also might want to control lease negotiation if there is a shortage of good locations. When good spots are in short supply, you need to make sure that you control access to those locations more than when good locations for your outlets are very common. By controlling the locations when the desirable locations are in short supply, you get another level of control over your franchisees. Having control over the best locations for a particular type of business provides a way to ensure that your franchisees conform to the rules of your system, to ensure that they are not terminated. Even if the system is not sufficiently valuable to get them to conform to stay in the system, they will do so to stay in the valuable spot if you control their leases and can force them to move out of their locations if they fail to conform.

> ## Stop! Don't Do It!
>
> 1. Don't ignore site-selection assistance as a way to help control your franchisees.
> 2. Don't provide lease-negotiation assistance when you first establish your franchise system; initially, you are better off not providing it.

Financing Franchisees

A final area of franchisee support that you should consider when establishing your franchise system is financing. Financing franchisees involves both direct and indirect financial assistance. Indirect financing involves assisting your franchisees in the process of obtaining capital from third parties—things such as providing introductions to lenders or helping with loan applications. Direct financing means providing money to franchisees.

Whereas many franchisors provide indirect financing assistance, only about one-third of them finance franchisees directly.[11] The most common form of direct financing is for the franchisor to take a promissory note for the franchise fee. Most evidence suggests that franchisors should not engage in direct financing—at least, not until they become large, public corporations with access to a large amount of capital.

One of the most valuable tools that franchisors have in finding the right franchisees is the ability to get potential franchisees to self-select. Because franchisees have to invest their own money in purchasing an outlet, only people who are truly able and confident in their abilities buy franchises and seek to capture a return that is dependent on their capabilities. If franchisors finance their franchisees, they undermine this selection mechanism and make it much harder to find good franchisees.

In contrast to the costs of directly financing franchisees, the costs of indirectly financing them are not very high, and the benefits are fairly large. So indirect financing makes a lot of sense for franchisors, particularly those who see franchisees with limited net worth as people with many other attributes that they want in their franchisees. For instance, a fast food franchisor seeking to establish more outlets in inner-city locations might see franchisees from inner cities as having the right knowledge of the market to be appropriate franchisees for those locations. If inner-city residents lack the net worth to qualify for franchises in those spots, helping them to get financing to buy the outlets would be a good strategy.

Stop! Don't Do It!

1. Don't directly finance franchise fees; it undermines the self-selection mechanism that helps you to identify the best franchisees.

Questions to Ask Yourself

1. How much and what type of training should I provide to franchisees? Should I offer some field training after the franchisees are already in operation?

2. Which support services should I offer to my franchisees? When should I first offer them?

3. Should I offer site-selection and lease-negotiation assistance to my franchisees?

4. Should I offer either direct or indirect financing to my franchisees?

Summary

This chapter discussed four categories of support and assistance that you need to consider offering to your franchisees: training; ongoing support services, such as centralized data processing and inventory control; real estate services (for the vast majority of franchise systems that have physical locations); and financing. To be successful, you must offer enough of the right type of support to attract franchisees, without offering so much support to attract the wrong type of franchisees.

To succeed, you need to offer your franchisees initial training in how to operate your business. Because training is costly, however, you must offer just the right amount, location, and timing of training: not so little that your franchisees cannot learn how to operate your business, and not so much that the training is too costly.

Your success also depends on your approach to support services. You need to balance the benefits of field operations evaluation in controlling franchisee behavior with the cost of undertaking this activity. You need to balance the benefits that come from centralizing services and establishing communication mechanisms with the expense of providing these things. In many cases, you may not want to provide these services initially, instead concentrating on selling franchises and establishing your brand name, and adopt these services when your system is larger and older.

Because many franchised businesses operate out of physical locations, you need to determine whether to provide real estate services to your franchisees. Site-selection assistance helps you to identify and control the right locations for your outlets. Similarly, lease-negotiation assistance provides you with an additional revenue source and a tool for controlling franchisee behavior. However, the benefits of these two activities might not outweigh their costs initially, so it might not be wise to adopt them until your system has grown from its initial starting point.

Finally, you need to consider whether to provide your franchisees with direct or indirect financing. Because the costs of indirect financing are not very high and its benefits are significant, indirect financing makes a great deal of sense for franchisors. Direct financing, however, makes less sense because it undermines the benefits of self-selection in identifying talented franchisees.

Now that you understand the issues that you will confront in deciding the type and level of support services to offer franchisees, we turn to a discussion of the territorial strategies for your franchise system.

7

TERRITORIAL STRATEGIES

To be successful as a franchisor, you need to determine the right strategy toward managing geographical territories. As was explained in earlier chapters, franchising tends to occur in industries in which sales and profit growth come from the addition of outlets to the system rather than the expansion of operations at existing locations. Consequently, figuring out how to expand the geographic reach of the system is crucial to success. If you adopt the wrong territorial strategy, you will almost certainly hinder your franchising efforts and might undermine an otherwise productive system. But the right territorial strategy is far from easy to determine.

In general, an effective territorial strategy has three broad components. The first involves deciding whether to engage in multiunit franchising. You need to determine whether you will engage master franchising, area development agreements, or subfranchising, all mechanisms to add more than one outlet at a time, or whether will you sell single outlets to franchisees. The second component involves what kind of territory to offer to your franchisees. Specifically, you need to figure out whether to provide franchisees with exclusive territories. If so, you need to determine the size of those territories. The third component of an effective strategy involves deciding whether to let your franchisees expand in their territories.

Of course, territorial strategies are complementary with some of the other policies described in earlier chapters. So another part of adopting your territorial strategy is figuring out what the right system policies are and ensuring that your territorial strategy fits those policies. This chapter offers specific information to help you assess the right approach to the dimensions of territorial strategy both individually and in conjunction with the other parts of the franchise system that you are developing.

Multiunit Franchising

Although the popular conception of franchising is that franchisors always sell individual units to franchisee owner-operators, this approach is but one way to approach franchising. Another way adopted by many franchisors is to use one of three versions of multiunit franchising: master franchising, area development, or subfranchising. To be successful at franchising, you need to figure out when, if at all, you should engage in multiunit franchising and, if so, which version to adopt.

Master Franchising

Master franchising is an arrangement in which the franchisor sells to another party (the master franchisee) the right to collect some portion of the up-front franchise fee and ongoing royalties in return for recruiting, training, and supporting the franchisees. Master franchising offers several advantages to you, the franchisor. The most important of these is accelerating the rate of growth of your franchise system by allowing you to establish outlets with very few headquarters personnel. Because someone else recruits, trains, and supports franchisees, your system can grow very quickly if you use master franchising. Wendy's, for instance, used this strategy to grow from 2 units to 1,400 units in only nine years.[1]

Master franchising also reduces the conflict between franchisors and franchisees that occurs with the addition of outlets to the system. As was discussed in Chapter 3, "The Disadvantages of Franchising," franchisors and franchisees face a fundamental conflict over the number of outlets that should be established in a geographical area because franchisors maximize system-wide sales and franchisees maximize outlet-level profits. Because master franchisees also seek to maximize sales, their goals are more closely aligned with those of the franchisor than with the goals of individual franchisees. If you use master franchising, you put yourself in the position of negotiating with someone whose goals are more closely aligned with your own when deciding to add outlets. Thus, using a master franchisee helps you to minimize the degree of direct conflict with your franchisees over market saturation. Because this type of conflict often spills over into other aspects of the franchisor-franchisee relationship, the use of master franchising can help you to reduce the adverse effects of conflict on system operations.

Master franchising also facilitates the buyback of franchised outlets because there are fewer parties with whom you must negotiate to repurchase outlets. If your strategy is to franchise temporarily to build a large chain and you lack the capital and human resources to build this chain through company-owned outlets, master franchising might be right for you. Master franchising permits the very rapid growth of the chain. Then, once the chain has been built, master franchising permits you to negotiate with one master franchisee to strike the terms of your deal to buy back outlets, which makes it relatively easy to regain control of them.

Finally, master franchising provides an effective way to obtain a partner with information about markets that you do not understand. This is one reason why master franchising is very popular when franchisors expand into foreign markets, where they often lack a good understanding of the local culture, economy, or legal system. By providing you with this expertise, the master franchisee allows you to select franchisees more effectively and to modify your system to the local market more appropriately.

Despite these benefits of master franchising, it is not a very good approach for most franchisors. In fact, master franchising is particularly problematic for new franchisors, which tend to be the very franchisors most likely to adopt this organizational arrangement. Research shows that new franchise systems that engage in master franchising are less likely than other franchise systems to survive over time.[2] Why? First off, by using master franchising, you give up an important carrot to encourage proper franchisee behavior. To keep franchisees in line, many franchisors offer new outlets to only those franchisees that follow system rules, which is a powerful incentive in profitable systems. However, if you engage in master franchising, you forfeit your right to pick the franchisees that get the rights to purchase additional outlets, undermining a key incentive that keeps them in line.

Master franchising also exacerbates the problem of selecting effective franchisees. To be successful, you have to choose the right franchisees. Of course, picking successful businesspeople from a pool of strangers isn't easy, and you will probably be wrong at least some of the time. With master franchising, you pick one partner, so the magnitude of the problem of picking a loser master franchisee is much greater than that of picking a loser individual franchisee.[3]

Finally, it is very difficult to develop realistic plans and proper incentives for master franchisees. To sign a contract with a master franchisee, you need to be able to specify, in advance, the quota of units that the master franchisee will need to sell and support. Not only does this approach create an incentive for your master franchisee to focus on selling franchises rather than on building the system, but also it assumes that you have an idea of what the right quota should be. If you are developing a new business in a new market, you might not actually know an appropriate number of franchises for the master franchisee to sell in that market. Many franchisors have run into trouble setting unrealistic quotas for the master franchisee without an understanding of what the market could bear.

Area Development

An area development agreement is a contract to provide a franchisee with the right to develop a territory that would hold more than one outlet. For example, you might offer a franchisee the right to all outlets in the state of Texas or in the country of Mexico.

Area development agreements are relatively uncommon in franchising. A recent survey showed that only 28 percent of franchisors offer area development agreements.[4] These agreements are more common in some industries than in others, but industry is not the only determinant of whether area development is used. Competing firms in the same industry often adopt different strategies toward area development. For instance, Bath Fitter®, a South Burlington, Vermont, franchisor of bathroom-remodeling services, seeks area developers; whereas its competitor, Bathcrest™, out of Salt Lake City, Utah, does not.[5] Therefore, you need to determine whether area development is something that fits your franchising strategy. That, of course, requires an understanding of the pros and cons of area development agreements.

One major advantage of area development agreements is that they reduce the number of franchisees that you need to attract to your system. Finding 1 good franchisee in a region is likely to be less expensive than finding 20 good franchisees, especially because the rewards of area development are greater than those for operating a single outlet.[6] If it is hard to find good franchisees, using area development agreements will allow you to expand more quickly and cheaply than you otherwise would.

Another major advantage of area development is that area franchisees can achieve economies of scale at the minichain level because their operations extend beyond a single outlet. For activities such as developing policies for the supervision of employees or investing in computer equipment, these scale economies can save money. Therefore, using area development agreements can make your franchise system more attractive to franchisees by improving their profit margins.

Similarly, area development provides the benefit of knowledge transfer from one outlet to another because solutions that the area franchisee learns can be applied in multiple outlets.[7] Chapter 3 explained that one of the disadvantages of franchising is that individual franchisees have neither the incentive nor the opportunity to transfer expertise that they have developed to other locations. However, an area franchisee has both the incentive and the opportunity to transfer knowledge learned from operating one outlet to another within the same area.

Finally, the free riding disadvantage of franchising is minimized when franchisees have areas to develop. Franchisees have an incentive to free-ride off of each other, not off of themselves. So if your franchise system requires a lot of advertising in a particular geographic market to generate customer demand for the product, each of your franchisees in the market will have an incentive to free-ride off of the efforts of the others to pay for advertising. However, if one franchisee has the rights to an entire area that is also a single advertising market—say, Atlanta—that franchisee won't free-ride on advertising. Because the franchisee runs all of the outlets in the media market, he or she will benefit from all the advertising done in that market and will have no incentive to free-ride.

The benefits of area development just described come at a cost. First, area development creates a shirking problem. Area franchisees must hire employees to run the outlets that they establish. As a result, the people running the outlets must be compensated from salaries, not from profits from running their outlets. This compensation scheme gives them an incentive to shirk, which Chapter 2, "The Advantages of Franchising," explained is one of the reasons to franchise in the first place. Moreover, systems that use area development end up creating hierarchies run by franchisees that look very similar to company-owned outlet chains, with all of the disadvantages that those hierarchies entail.

Another disadvantage of area development is that it increases the power that your franchisees have over you. In place of a system in which you have many small franchisees, area development gives you a system with a few large franchisees. It is easier for you to negotiate with your franchisees if you have a larger number of small franchisees than if you have a smaller number of larger franchisees. In the case of the former, you will not suffer as much from the decision of any one franchisee to act counter to your interests than you will in the case of the latter. Therefore, your bargaining position is much stronger if you have a large number of small franchisees than if you have a small number of large franchisees.

Subfranchising

Subfranchising is a strategy in which a franchisor sells someone the rights to resell outlets to franchisees. Figure 7.1 shows the structure of a subfranchising arrangement. With this arrangement, the subfranchisor becomes responsible for training the franchisees, setting them up in operation, and collecting royalties.[8]

Of course, not all franchisors engage in subfranchising. For instance, Arabica Coffee House, a franchisor of coffee shops out of Independence, Ohio, permits subfranchising, whereas its competitor,

Gloria Jean's® Coffees, out of Irvine, California, does not.[9] To determine whether subfranchising is something that you want to do, you need to develop an understanding of the pros and cons of this arrangement.

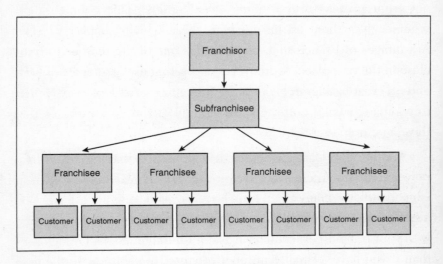

FIGURE 7.1   A Typical Subfranchising Structure

On the positive side, subfranchising enhances growth. With the subfranchisor identifying franchisees, supporting them, monitoring their activities, and collecting royalties, you can set up a much larger span of control for your headquarters staff and grow larger with fewer people if you engage in subfranchising than if you do not. This effect on growth is the primary benefit of subfranchising.

Although subfranchising enables you to grow your business faster for a given investment in human and physical capital than you can by direct franchising, it tends to be a poor strategy for franchisors to follow most of the time. By using this arrangement, you create partners with significant power over you because subfranchisors account for more revenue and operate more outlets than individual outlet operators.[10] Thus, negotiations with subfranchisors are much more difficult than negotiations with individual franchisees, putting the franchisor at a disadvantage.

In addition, for subfranchising to work, franchisors need to specify the franchise development schedule. The need to establish the development schedule creates a similar problem to the one described earlier about establishing a development schedule for master franchisees. As a franchisor, you will likely expect your subfranchisor to be able to identify franchisees faster than the subfranchisor thinks that he or she can. This will make it difficult for you and your subfranchisor to come to an agreement about the right development schedule for your system.

A last disadvantage of subfranchising concerns the difficulty of identifying qualified subfranchisors. Many times, the financial demands on a subfranchisor are higher than on most individual franchisees. Relatively few people who want to operate a subfranchise have the several million dollars that it takes to obtain a subfranchise in many systems. Therefore, if you choose to go the subfranchising route, you might end up wasting a lot of your time looking for subfranchisors when few are available.

Stop! Don't Do It!

1. Don't use master franchising when you first establish your franchise system if you are worried about selecting the right franchisees or controlling their behavior.

2. Don't use area development if you are worried about powerful franchisees or shirking by outlet operators.

3. Don't use sub-franchising if you are unsure of what the right development schedule for outlet growth should be.

Right to Expand

Another aspect of territorial strategy that you need to consider when you set up you franchise system is whether to offer your franchisees the right to expand in their territories before you offer franchises to people currently outside the system. Most franchisors offer their franchisees this right. In fact, some systems are quite reliant on expansion by existing franchisees for their growth. For instance, more than 60 percent of new outlets in the McDonald's system are established by franchisees that are already in the system.[11]

In general, allowing existing franchisees the opportunity to expand by acquiring new outlets is a good strategy. If your franchisees know that they have the right to add outlets, they will have an incentive to adhere to the rules of the system. This makes monitoring them much easier. If you use field audit scores as a mechanism for deciding who should be allowed to have additional outlets, your franchisees will strive to obtain the high scores necessary to expand.

Allowing franchisees to add outlets also allows you to grow at relatively low cost in terms of recruiting, selecting, and training new franchisees. In more than three quarters of all franchise systems, when existing franchisees add outlets, they pay the same franchise fee and agree to the same royalty rate as new franchisees.[12] However, when existing franchisees purchase additional outlets, you, the franchisor, don't need to incur additional costs to select the franchisees. You have already done that. Moreover, existing franchisees tend not to demand as many support services as new franchisees when they open the new outlets. So, if your existing franchisees add outlets, you will spend less on support services than if new franchisees open the outlets.

Allowing existing franchisees to expand in their territories is also a way to minimize encroachment problems that lead to conflict in franchise systems. As you should remember from Chapter 3, one of the problems of franchising is that franchisees fear that new locations will cannibalize some of their sales, making their outlets less profitable. Although your franchisees might prefer that no additional outlets get established at all, they will prefer owning the additional outlets that you establish to having those outlets go to someone else. If existing franchisees have the right to establish the new outlets, they might be able to gain some economies across the outlets, mitigating the adverse effects of market saturation on the performance of their original outlets.

Some franchisors adopt just this approach of giving existing franchisees the right to buy all new outlets that the franchisor is establishing in the area near their existing outlets. For example, Great Clips®, a hair care franchise out of Minneapolis, Minnesota, has established a policy of giving its franchisees a right of first refusal on all new locations.[13] The founders of Great Clips believe that this approach reduces the level of conflict between themselves and their franchisees over market saturation.

Stop! Don't Do It!

1. Don't try to sell additional outlets to new franchisees when you have high-performing franchisees eager to expand.
2. Don't forget that giving franchisees the right to expand in their territories is a powerful incentive to perform.

Exclusive Territories

Franchisors often provide franchisees with an exclusive territory, or a geographic location within which the franchisor agrees not to add a company-owned outlet or to sell an outlet to another franchisee. In fact, 70 percent of franchisors offer exclusive territories to their franchisees.[14]

Providing your franchisees with exclusive territories tends to be a good strategy, especially if your system is new or small. Exclusive territories are more valuable when franchisees are relatively more important to the system, which is true early in the chain's life. When the product or service that the franchisor sells is new and customers do not know much about it, franchisee efforts are very important for selling to end customers. Over time, when the product becomes better known to customers, the efforts of the franchisor to guarantee quality and promote the brand name become more important for sales than franchisee efforts, and exclusive territories, while valuable, become less important.[15]

Research supports this argument. In a study of 170 new franchise systems founded in the early 1990s conducted with Pierre Azoulay of Columbia University, I found that 91 percent of new franchise systems that survived over time offered franchisees exclusive territories, in contrast to only 31 percent of new franchise systems that did not offer exclusive territories.

Why is it a good strategy for you to provide your franchisees with exclusive territories? After all, exclusive territories have a cost. Because franchisees seek to maximize profits, but franchisors seek to maximize sales, franchisees will not want as many outlets in an area as you would like to create. Therefore, you cannot saturate the market with as many outlets as you would like if you offer franchisees exclusive territories.

However, exclusive territories provide many benefits that offset this cost. First, exclusive territories make your franchisees less worried that you will threaten to put new outlets in their geographic areas as a way to extract a greater share of profits from their operations. Opportunistic franchisors could threaten to add outlets right next door to their existing franchisees unless the franchisees agreed to pay higher royalty rates. Franchisee fears that you will engage in such efforts to opportunistically renegotiate the terms of their franchise agreements are alleviated by exclusive territories that keep this opportunistic activity from taking place.

Exclusive territories also minimize competition between outlets within the chain for the same customers. Antitrust laws preclude franchisors from telling franchisees where they can and cannot sell their products and services, so franchisees of the same chain can and do compete with each other. Franchisors would like to minimize this competition, which reduces overall sales. Offering an exclusive geographic area to a franchisee greatly minimizes the level of this within chain competition, if a business—say, a sign shop—depends on having a fixed location. People will travel only so far to buy a sign. If you give one franchisee the exclusive right to a particular geographic area (that is, a particular city), it is unlikely that he or she will face competition from other franchisees in another geographic area.

Although it is clearly valuable for you to offer exclusive territories to your franchisees, you also need to decide on the size of those territories. For instance, East Coast Original Frozen Custard offers its franchisees an exclusive territory for a 5-mile radius from the outlet.

How large of a territory you should offer your franchisees depends, in part, on the nature of your industry. A fast food restaurant might be quite profitable if it has an exclusive territory of a few city blocks, particularly in a densely populated place such as Manhattan. However, an office-cleaning business might need an entire city as a territory, or the franchisee will be unable to make a go of it.

Deciding how large of an exclusive territory to offer your franchisees is difficult because it is possible to offer your franchisees too large of an exclusive territory. Not only will offering territories that are too large lower the density of outlets in your system and, hence, the profitability of your operation, but it also will allow other companies to move into the area and compete with you.

For instance, suppose that you have given exclusive rights to the Cleveland, Ohio, market of your auto-repair franchise to one franchisee with one location. Your major competitor could move in and establish ten outlets in the city, while you are locked into one location. Because you have given too large of an exclusive territory to your franchisee, you will have to compete with another chain that gets better scale economies on advertising its business and has more locations available to the customers to whom you are both trying to sell.

A last thought that you want to consider with exclusive territories is how to measure the size of the exclusive area that you provide. Depending on the nature of your product or service, the right way to measure size of the territory might be the size of the geographic area, the number of people in that area, or their wealth or income. For example, the right size of an exclusive territory for a children's education class might be better determined by the number of children in a part of town than by square mileage.

> ## Stop! Don't Do It!
>
> 1. Don't focus too much on outlet density; you need to give franchisees exclusive territories to attract them to your system.
> 2. Don't make your exclusive territories too large, or your competitors develop a better competitive position in the market than you.

Complements

As was explained in Chapter 5, "Key Franchising Policies," complements are things that work better when they are jointly adopted than they are used individually. Several aspects of your territorial strategy will be complementary with other policies that you adopt. Therefore, you will want to consider the complementary relationship between franchisee territories and other policies, and factor these in when evaluating your approach to franchisee territories. For instance, exclusive territories and minimum expansion requirements are complementary. That is, you want to make sure you adopt policies that set minimum expansion plans for your franchisees if you are going to give them exclusive territories. The idea here is that you need to encourage franchisee effort if you are giving franchisees exclusive territories that can be developed only by them.[16] This is only one example, but it illustrates the importance of thinking about franchise system policies and territorial strategies as complementary and worthy of joint evaluation.

Questions to Ask Yourself
1.   Should I sell one outlet at a time or use multiunit franchising?
2.   Should I give my franchisees exclusive territories? If so, how large should those territories be?
3.   Should I allow my franchisees to expand by adding outlets in their territories?
4.   What policies should I adopt to complement my territorial strategy?

Summary

This chapter discussed three key dimensions of territorial strategy that, you, the franchisor, need to consider: whether to engage in multiunit franchising, what kind of territory to offer to your franchisees, and whether to let your existing franchisees expand in their territories. To be successful, you must adopt the right territorial strategy. Otherwise, you can undermine an otherwise productive system, turning a winning franchise into a losing one.

The first part of a successful territorial strategy involves deciding whether to engage in multiunit franchising, the sale of more than one outlet to your franchisees. Three different kinds of multiunit franchising exist: master franchising, area development, and subfranchising.

Master franchising is an arrangement in which the franchisor sells to another party—the master franchisee—the right to collect some portion of the up front-franchise fee and ongoing royalties in return for recruiting, training, and supporting franchisees. Master franchising enhances system growth, reduces conflict between franchisors and franchisees that results from the addition of outlets to the system, facilitates the buyback of outlets, and provides an efficient way of finding a partner with local market knowledge. However, on average, master franchising is not a very good strategy. It hinders quality control, undermines franchisee incentives, exacerbates the problems of selecting the wrong partners, and creates unrealistic development plans with poor incentives.

Area development is a policy of giving a franchisee the right to develop a territory that would hold more than one outlet. Area development is effective at controlling franchisee free riding, reduces the number of franchisees that you need to identify, and helps to achieve scale economies and knowledge transfer at the franchisee level. However, these benefits come at the expense of ownership incentives as a solution to outlet-level shirking and increased franchisee power.

Subfranchising is a strategy in which a franchisor sells to a franchisee the rights to resell outlets to franchisees. Although it spurs system growth, subfranchising also causes several problems: conflict over the system development schedule, reduced leverage over negotiating partners, and a smaller pool of qualified buyers.

The second part of an effective territorial strategy involves deciding whether to offer existing franchisees the right to expand in their territories. In general, this is a wise strategy because it provides franchisees with an incentive to adhere to the rules of the system, reduces the costs of establishing additional outlets, and minimizes encroachment problems.

The third part of an effective territorial strategy concerns providing franchisees with an exclusive territory. Even though offering exclusive territories reduces the level of market saturation that your franchise system can achieve, it tends to be a good strategy, particularly in new systems. Offering exclusive territories reduces franchisee free riding, makes franchisees less worried about encroachment, and minimizes competition within the system.

However, you do not want to offer exclusive territories that are too large. Oversized territories will reduce your profits by lowering your outlet density, allowing your competitors a better position than you in the market place.

Finally, as with many of the policies that were discussed in Chapter 5, territorial strategies are complementary with many system policies. Therefore, you should consider the fit between your territorial strategy and your system policies to make sure that they are aligned when you establish both of these.

Now that you understand the key issues in creating a territorial strategy, we turn to pricing the franchise system, which is the subject of the next chapter.

8

PRICING FRANCHISES

To be successful as a franchisor, you need to price your franchises correctly. If you charge your franchisees too much, they will not buy into the system. If you charge them too little, you are leaving money on the table that you could take home in the form of profit.

As a franchisor, you need to consider two basic components to pricing your franchise: the up-front franchise fee and the ongoing royalty rate. Unfortunately, most franchisors don't know how to set their franchise fees or royalty rates. One franchisor that I interviewed told me he set his royalty rate at 5 percent of sales because the number "had a nice ring to it." Another franchisor told me that he set his franchise fee at $20,000 because that was "a round number." Rather than using these types of heuristics to set your royalty rate and franchise fee, you are better off using some systematic logic.

This chapter offers specific information to help you determine the right franchise fee and royalty rate for your system. It explains how to incorporate information about your industry, product offering, territorial strategy, intellectual property, operating system, and franchisee support services to come up with the right price for your franchised outlets. The chapter also explains how franchise fees and royalty rates should change as your franchise system matures and grows.

Franchise Fee

The franchise fee is a one-time payment made by the franchisee to the franchisor when the franchise agreement is executed. The purpose of the franchise fee is to compensate you, the franchisor, for the cost of getting the franchisee started in business; it includes the value of goodwill, the value of the franchisee's territory, the cost of identifying and training franchisees, location assistance, and the costs of signage and other initial equipment provided by the franchisor.[1]

According to a survey of franchisors made by the International Franchise Association, the average initial franchise fee is approximately $32,000.[2] However, the fees vary significantly across industries, ranging from an average of $19,000 for travel agencies to $111,000 for sports-related franchises. Table 8.1 shows the average franchise fees in selected industries.

TABLE 8.1   Average Franchise Fees in Selected Industries

Industry	Average Franchise Fee
Lodging	$35,200
Restaurants	$31,900
Printing and copying	$27,900
Security and safety systems	$27,100
Hair care	$25,200
Employment and personnel services	$22,700
Auto repair	$22,600
Business services	$22,194
Fast food	$20,800
Laundry and dry cleaning	$19,000
Real estate	$14,700
Travel agencies	$14,000

Source: Adapted from data in R. Bond's *Bond's Franchise Guide* (Oakland, CA: Sourcebook Publications, 2004).

A variety of other factors also influence the franchise fee that you, as a franchisor, can charge. The value of the system brand name, the production process, franchisee profiles, outlet profit margins, and industry norms are among the factors that influence the size of the franchise fee. You can charge a higher franchise fee if your franchise system is larger and has operated for a longer period of time because franchise fees incorporate the value of goodwill, which is higher if you have more experience and more outlets.[3] When you establish a new franchise system, you should charge relatively low franchise fees in comparison to the McDonald's and Subways of the world because you do not yet have as strong a brand name as these companies.

Another factor that affects the size of the franchise fee that you can charge is the value of the geographical territory that you are providing to the franchisee. When franchisees receive larger territories for a given type of product or service, they expect to pay larger fees. After all, they are getting the right to sell a product or service to more customers. And, of course, the fees will be higher if those territories are exclusive. Franchisees are willing to pay a premium for your commitment not to sell an outlet to someone else in the same geographic area.

The cost, extent, and type of services that you are providing to your franchisees also affect the size of the franchise fee that you can charge. As was discussed in the last chapter, much of what franchisors do for their franchisees occurs before the outlet is set up. For instance, the franchisor selects the franchisees and helps to identify the locations, set up the outlets, and provides training and assistance in operating the outlets. It stands to reason that the greater the expenses that you incur in selecting your franchisees and the more up-front assistance and training that you provide to them, the higher the franchise fee is that you can charge. If you offer a more complex operation that requires more training than other franchisors, or if you offer site selection, field assistance at startup, or other services, you can charge a higher franchise fee.

The term of your franchise contract also affects the initial fee that you charge your franchisees. Essentially, the longer the term of the contract is, the higher the fee is that you can charge; the franchisee can amortize the fee over a larger period of time if the contract term is longer. For instance, if you are willing to sign a 20-year contract for your sports club franchise, you can charge a higher fee than if you are willing to sign only a two-year contract for the same franchise.

Over time, you should increase your franchise fees to reflect increased expenses that you face. As the services that you provide to your franchisees increase in cost because of inflation or other factors, you should be able to pass on these increases to your franchisees. In addition, you will be more likely to add services for your franchisees than take them away, which will also allow you to charge higher franchise fees over time. Furthermore, the value of your brand name should increase, permitting you to increase your franchise fee to reflect this greater value.[4] Therefore, you should be able to increase your franchise fee as your system matures. However, you need to have reasonable expectations about the magnitude of increases in your franchise fee. Even if your system is very successful, you probably will be able to increase your franchise fee only a couple of points over the rate of inflation. Because of the complexities of increasing franchise fees for new franchisees while keeping them the same for existing franchisees, franchise fees are very sticky; they change slowly and by small amounts over time.

On average, the up-front franchise fee that your franchisees will pay is 8 percent of the value of all payments that they will make to you over the life of your franchise agreement.[5] Although there is certainly some variation across franchise systems in the size of this percentage, it rarely comes close to the entire lifetime cost of the franchise. Why not? If you charged your franchisees the entire cost of the franchise up front, you would have no incentive to continue to support the system over time. Franchisees know the basic economics of this situation and would not buy into a franchise system that receives almost all of its compensation through an up-front fee, for fear that the franchisor would abandon them.

Moreover, if you received all of your fees up front, you would have a strong incentive to opportunistically terminate your franchisees and collect another round of fees by reselling the outlet. I'm not saying that you would do this—your ethics might preclude it. But the strength of that incentive will scare away a lot of franchisees, most of whom don't know you or your ethics and would be afraid of this potential opportunism.

A third reason that you will receive a small franchise fee relative to the total size of payments franchisees will make to you over the life of the franchise agreement is that your franchisees are unlikely to be able to pay for the entire price of the outlet up front. Most people who buy franchises have limited capital. Typically, they need to use up much of their savings, borrow money from friends and family, or raise capital from financial institutions just to cover the initial opening costs for the franchises that they buy. As a result, the ability of most franchisees to pay the entire price of the outlet up front, particularly in high-cost industries such as restaurants and lodging, is very low. Therefore, you—and franchisors like you—will be able to charge franchisees only a small portion of the total cost of a franchise up front in the form of the franchise fee.

Stop! Don't Do It!

1. Don't try to capture too much of the cost of your franchise system through your up-front fee; you will have trouble attracting franchisees.

2. Don't charge too low of a fee given your industry, level of brand name reputation, and support that you are providing to franchisees.

Royalty Rate

The second major component of the price of a franchise system is the ongoing royalty paid to franchisors by franchisees. As a franchisor, the royalty is your major source of compensation, often accounting for more than 90 percent of the money that you receive from your franchisees over the life of your franchise agreement. In addition to providing you with your profit, the royalty gives you the incentive (and capital) to support the franchise system over time. Royalties will be used to support your efforts to build the system, to pay for ongoing training, to help existing franchisees work out the kinks in their operations, to develop the brand name, to develop new products and services, and to monitor your franchisees.

You should not underestimate the importance of ongoing royalties as a source of funds for further development of your business. The magnitude of the expenses that you are likely to incur as you develop new products or services for your franchisees over time might surprise you. For instance, McDonald's spent $3 million in 1960s dollars just perfecting its French fry cooking method and type of potato used![6] That translates to tens of millions of today's dollars to develop just a single product. The message here is not to view your royalties as pure profit, but to think of some of those payments as money to be reinvested in your business. To have the money to invest in the development of the business and to earn a reasonable profit, you might need to charge a higher royalty than you initially envisage.

When you set up your franchise system, you will also need to decide how you will charge royalties. Although you have a variety of options, most franchisors charge a royalty on the gross sales of products by their franchisees. Only 5 percent of franchisors charge a flat royalty rate, with the most common arrangement being a percentage of gross sales, preferred by 82 percent of franchisors. Of those charging a percentage royalty rate, 93 percent take that percentage on sales.[7]

Why charge royalties as a percentage of sales rather than a percentage of profits? One reason is that you can affect your franchisees' sales much more easily than you can affect their profits. Therefore, royalties on gross sales provide a better incentive to you, and other franchisors like you, than royalties on gross profits. If you charge royalties on gross sales, you will be highly motivated to help maximize your franchisees' performance at selling the system's product or service.

Perhaps a more important reason for charging a royalty on sales is that monitoring sales is easier than monitoring profits. Profits are much easier to manipulate than sales because franchisees can reduce their profits by adjusting their costs upward. By collecting royalties on sales, franchisors can ignore any manipulations to costs that franchisees might make to reduce their profits. They need to keep track of only the top line in franchisee operations. Although this is not exactly easy, it is much more doable than keeping track of royalties on profits.

Charging a royalty on sales also reduces franchisor risk relative to charging a royalty on profits because outlets vary more in their profit performance than in their sales performance. Because performance variation results from both changes in sales and changes in costs, sales variation is lower than profit variation. Therefore, you can reduce your risk as a franchisor by charging royalties on sales rather than by charging royalties on profits.[8]

In addition to deciding what you charge a royalty on, you need to decide the rate that your franchisees need to pay. The most common percentage royalty, charged by roughly a third of franchisors, is 4 to 5 percent of sales. For example, Big Apple Bagels®, a franchised bagel bakery out of Chicago, changes its franchisees a 5 percent royalty on gross sales.[9] But the royalty rates that franchisors charge range from 1 percent to 50 percent of gross sales.

So what royalty rate should you charge? Your industry will determine a lot of the answer to this question. The nature of profit margins in your industry, the type of products that you sell, the abilities of franchisees in your business, their need for assistance, and the cost of monitoring them all affect royalty rates. For instance, if you are in a business with very narrow margins, you will have to settle for a smaller royalty than if you are in a business with fatter margins. You cannot charge too high of a royalty rate because your royalty rate reduces your franchisees' profits. If your franchisees earn very little profit, they will lose all of their incentive to perform. One rule of thumb in franchising is to make sure that the royalties that you charge do not exceed one-third of the franchisees' profits before paying royalties. Table 8.2 shows the average royalty rates for selected industries.

TABLE 8.2   Average Royalty Rates in Selected Industries

Industry	Average Royalty Rate
Business services	10.6%
Employment and personnel services	6.5%
Printing and copying	5.9%
Hair care	5.2%
Auto repair	5.0%
Security and safety systems	4.9%
Real estate	4.8%
Fast food	4.7%
Restaurants	4.5%
Laundry and dry cleaning	4.5%
Lodging	4.2%
Travel agencies	0.4%

Source: Adapted from data in R. Bond's *Bond's Franchise Guide* (Oakland, CA: Sourcebook Publications, 2004).

But the margins of your business are not the only thing that affects your royalty rate. After all, firms in the same industry that produce the same product often charge their franchisees different royalty rates. For example, Dunkin' Donuts® charges a royalty rate of 5.9 percent of gross sales; whereas its competitor Robin's Donuts charges a royalty rate of only 4 percent of gross sales.[10]

The royalty rate that you charge should reflect the relative contributions that you and your franchisees make to the system. If your franchisees' contribution to the system is very high, as is the case when they have a great deal of valuable local market knowledge that you are using to develop the system, the royalty rate that you charge should be relatively low. In contrast, when your contribution, as the franchisor, is very large, as is the case when you have developed some sort of proprietary product or process that you are providing to your franchisees, the royalty rate that you charge should be relatively high.

Similarly, the level of ongoing support—things such as field training or centralized purchasing—that you provide to your franchisees affects your royalty rate. If you provide more services to your franchisees, you can expect your franchisees to pay a higher royalty rate than if you offer them relatively few services. Your royalty rate will have to be lower than that of competitors if they offer their franchisees inventory management, centralized data processing, and a host of other support functions and you do not.

Your royalty rate should also reflect the value of your system's brand name. One reason is that a strong brand name attracts customers to your franchisees' outlets, allowing them to make more sales at a lower cost and enhancing their profits. Another reason is that you, as a franchisor, need a stronger incentive to monitor the franchise system against free riding when the value of the brand name is higher. Because franchisee free riding increases with the value of the system brand name, franchisees are willing to pay more for protection against free riding by other franchisees as the system's brand becomes more valuable, allowing you, as a franchisor, to charge a higher royalty rate.

The more years that you have operated your business before franchising, the higher your royalty rates can be.[11] Not only will longer operations before franchising enhance the value of your brand name, but they will improve your operating system. Having moved further up the learning curve to create a more valuable operating system means that what you are offering to your franchisees is a better business operation, and they should be willing to pay more for that.

Although royalties account for the vast majority of the compensation that you will receive from your franchisees, you can also earn money from them in other ways. You need to think about where else you get your profits as a franchisor when you set your royalty rates. Some franchisors lease their land to franchisees and, therefore, obtain revenue from that activity. McDonald's, for example, marks up the rent paid on outlets that it rents to franchisees as another source of revenues. In the case of McDonald's, in fact, leasing real estate is actually a greater source of revenues from franchisees than the royalties that they pay for the use of the brand name and operating system.[12]

Other franchisors sell or lease specialized equipment necessary for producing the product or service provided to end customers or offer key required inputs to franchisees at a marked-up price. For instance, East Coast Original Frozen Custard requires its franchisees to purchase custard and yogurt mixes and machines for making the frozen desserts from the franchisor, allowing it to make a profit on the supply of those inputs. In fact, these alternative revenue sources for the franchisor may explain why the company charges its franchisees only a 1 percent royalty rate.

Because royalty rates are lower if franchisees earn money by charging their franchisees a margin on inputs, royalty rates are higher in service franchises than in product franchises. In franchises that sell products, the franchisor can make a portion of profits through the sale of goods to franchisees, an arrangement not possible with service franchises.[13]

A final factor that influences the royalties that you can charge your franchisees is their level of sales. You can charge higher royalty rates when the level of sales at your franchisee's outlets is higher than when it is lower. Why? Most franchisees seek to achieve an absolute level of compensation. If their sales are higher, they can afford a higher percentage of royalties and still make their target compensation. If your franchise focuses on locations or in industries with high sales volume, it can charge a higher royalty rate than competitor franchises.

Another issue that you need to consider in franchising your business is how often to collect your royalties. Approximately 54 percent of franchisors require royalties to be paid monthly, and 18 percent require them to be paid weekly.[14] The advantage of collecting royalties weekly, of course, is cash flow. It is quite possible to generate positive cash flow for your franchise by collecting your royalties weekly and paying most of your bills on a 30- or 90-day cycle. On the other hand, weekly royalty payments create cash-flow problems for your franchisees and might hinder their performance. You need to balance the benefits to you with the harm to them in setting the frequency of royalty payments.

Stop! Don't Do It!

1. Don't charge very high royalty rates if you can also earn margins on inputs sold to your franchisees.
2. Don't charge a high royalty rate if your system brand name is not well developed.
3. Don't charge a high royalty rate if you are not providing many services to your franchisees.

Relationship Between Franchise Fees and Royalty Rates

Royalty rates and franchisee fees both tend to be lower in young and small franchise systems than in older, more mature ones. This is because the price of a franchise reflects the underlying value to franchisees of being in the system. Because it is more valuable to be part of the McDonald's chain than to be a member of Scott's Hamburger Hut system, McDonald's can charge its franchisees more for access to its brand name and system assets. Therefore, as explained earlier, over time, franchisors tend to increase both their royalty rates and their franchise fees to reflect increases in the value of the system.

However, the relative shifts in franchise fees and royalty rates over time are not the same. New franchisors tend to discount their up-front fees more and set their royalty rates off the prices charged by the average franchisor in an industry. Because ongoing royalties depend on the value of the business format, but up-front franchise fees do not, new franchisors without established reputations can attract franchisees more easily by shifting payment for their business format from flat up-front fees to royalties as a percentage of sales to end users.

The use of this pricing arrangement reduces the franchisees' risk of selecting the wrong franchisors by minimizing the amount that they have to pay if the business format turns out to be of low value. With a very low royalty rate and a very high up-front franchise fee, the amount that the franchisee would have to pay for the business format would be largely independent of the value of the format. However, with a higher royalty rate and a lower up-front fee, the franchisee's payment to the franchisor is closely tied to the value of the business format in ensuring sales of products and services to the end customer. Because franchisees will find it less risky to select a franchisor that uses the pricing strategy of a relatively low franchise fee and a relatively high royalty rate, new franchisors that adopt this strategy will find it easier to attract the franchisees that they need to grow and so will be more likely to survive than other new franchisors.

Over time, these franchisors survive and grow. As they mature, they tend to increase their franchise fees faster than their royalty rates, redressing this balance between the two sources of franchisee payment as franchise systems become older and larger.

Stop! Don't Do It!

1. Don't charge high royalty rates and franchise fees in a new franchise system; you will not attract franchisees.

2. Don't take a large portion of your compensation from up-front fees when your franchise system is new; focus instead on getting this money from royalties.

Questions to Ask Yourself

1. How much should my up-front franchisee fee be?

2. How much should my royalty be?

3. Should I charge a flat rate or royalty as a percentage? Should the percentage be of franchisee gross sales or profits? Should it be collected monthly or weekly?

4. What portion of my compensation should I take from up-front fees and what portion from ongoing royalties?

5. How should I change the balance between my royalty rate and my franchise fees over time?

Summary

To be successful you must price your franchise system correctly. If you charge too high of a price, you will not attract franchisees. If you charge too low of a price, you are leaving money on the table and might not be able to pay for the further development of your system. This chapter discussed the two key dimensions of pricing a franchise system: the up-front franchise fee and the ongoing royalty.

The franchise fee is a one-time payment made by the franchisee to the franchisor at the time that the franchise agreement is executed, to compensate the franchisor for the cost of getting the franchisee started in business. On average, franchise fees represent about 8 percent of the total amount paid by the franchisee to the franchisor over the life of the agreement, or roughly $32,000. Your franchisee fee will be higher if you are in an industry with higher margins, if your business has a stronger brand name reputation, if the geographic territory you are offering to franchisees is larger, if you offer more franchisee services, and if the term of your contract is longer. Over time, most successful franchisors raise their franchise fees, although not by much more than the rate of inflation.

The royalty is an ongoing payment made by the franchisee to the franchisor, and it represents the major source of franchisor compensation. Royalty rates are designed to provide franchisors with a profit and to pay for efforts to further develop the system. Most franchisors charge royalties on gross sales because royalties on sales offer better incentives than royalties on profit, are easier to monitor, and cause franchisors to bear less risk than royalties on profits. Your royalty rate will be higher if you operate in an industry with higher profit margins; if your franchisees have higher sales volume; if your contributions are relatively more important to the success of the system; if you provide more support to franchisees; if your system has a stronger brand name; if your business has been in operation longer; and if you do not make profits through other means, such as leasing space to franchisees or selling them inputs at a profit.

Royalty rates and franchise fees both tend to be lower in new systems than in older ones because the price of a franchise system reflects the underlying value of the system to franchisees. However, new franchisors tend to discount their up-front fees more and their royalties less than the average franchisor in an industry because this arrangement reduces franchisees' risk of selecting the wrong system to enter.

Now that you understand the key issues in pricing a franchise, the next chapter covers a strategy for successful franchise system expansion.

9

EXPANSION STRATEGIES

Success in business often depends on your approach to expanding your operations. Because franchising tends to occur in businesses in which expansion can't occur at one location, but instead requires the addition of new outlets, this means that the magnitude of profits that you earn from franchising depends largely on how quickly and effectively you expand the number of locations where you serve customers. Done correctly, geographic expansion will increase the profits of your business dramatically; done incorrectly, it will undermine the profitability of your operation.

This chapter offers specific information to help you determine the right expansion strategy for your franchise system. As a franchisor, you need to make sure that you get five parts of an expansion strategy right:

- When in the life of your business to start franchising

- The right balance between franchised and company-owned outlets in your chain

- Which outlets to franchise and which to own

- How to expand geographically

- When and how to expand internationally

When Should You First Franchise?

Although you might be persuaded by what you have read in earlier chapters of this book and now believe that franchising is the right way to go, you should operate your business for several years before you begin to franchise. Most successful franchisors do not begin to franchise immediately upon starting their businesses. In fact, research shows that the older new franchisors are at the time that they begin franchising, the more likely those franchise systems are to survive over time.[1]

By operating for a while before franchising, you can develop an understanding of the keys to success in your industry before you try to pass on that knowledge to others. In addition, you can develop an understanding of the right system to put in place at the outlet level and can avoid using your franchisees as guinea pigs in unproven experiments.

You also increase the likelihood that you will be around to support your franchisees if you operate for a while before initiating franchising. The failure rate of firms goes down as they mature. Therefore, if you have been operating your business for a while before franchising, your likelihood of failure will be lower, and the likelihood that you will be able to support your franchisees will be higher than if you start franchising right when you start your business.

Of course, how long you need to operate to learn what it takes to be successful in your business and how long you need to wait before beginning to franchise depend on your industry. Table 9.1 provides information on the average number of years that franchisors are in operation before franchising for selected industries.

TABLE 9.1 Average Number of Years Franchisors are in Operation Before Franchising for Selected Industries

Industry	Years Before Franchising
Auto repair	5.9
Baked goods	6.9
Building and construction	5.1
Business services	4.5
Child related	3.8
Education related	12.0
Fast food	7.1
Lodging	11.9
Maintenance services	6.8
Personnel services	7.0
Real estate	10.8
Restaurants	9.3
Retail food	16.2
Retail	7.0
Services	4.3
Sports and recreation	2.9
Travel	1.8
Overall	**7.6**

Source: Adapted from data in the IFA Educational Foundation's *The Profile of Franchising* (Washington, DC: IFA, 1998).

Stop! Don't Do It!

1. Don't start to franchise as soon as you have started a business; operate your own outlets for several years to figure out how to run your business effectively.

2. Don't rely just on the averages; be sure to consider the length of time that firms in your industry need to operate before franchising.

How Many Outlets Should You Own?

Statistics show that mature franchisors tend to target less than one-fifth of their outlets to be company owned. In fact, on average, franchisees own roughly 84 percent of the outlets in franchise chains, and franchisors own 16 percent.[2]

However, these average statistics hide major strategic changes in the role of company-owned outlets over the life of the typical franchise system. As Figure 9.1 shows, the proportion of franchised outlets in franchise systems is initially very low, rises dramatically over the first few years of franchising, remains stable for a long period of time, and then exhibits a slight decline when systems become mature.

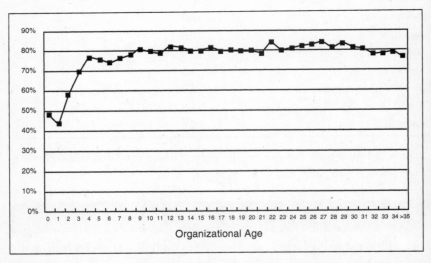

FIGURE 9.1   Proportion of Company-Owned Outlets in Franchise Systems by Organizational Age

The following sections outline the relative balance between franchised and company-owned outlets in franchise chains over the life of those chains. These sections focus on three key periods in the life of a franchise: when systems are new, when they are in a period of high growth, and when they are mature.

Company-Owned Outlets in New Franchisors

Most successful new franchisors begin with some company-owned outlets. These outlets—typically established during the period before your company began to franchise—are important to success at franchising because they provide evidence to franchisees that you, as a franchisor, have confidence in the value of your new system. As a franchisor, you cannot easily demonstrate the value of the new system that you are trying to sell to franchisees because its major asset, the business format, is intangible. For example, it is difficult to know whether the recipes of your new fast food chain will prove to be popular with consumers until someone has produced meals based on those recipes and has sold them successfully. The intangibility of the business format makes it hard for prospective franchisees to determine the value to them of buying your business format before purchasing it and so makes it hard to persuade prospective franchisees to buy a franchise from you.

Moreover, you cannot convince potential franchisees of the value of your system simply by claiming that your business format is valuable. All franchisors (those offering business formats that are valuable and those offering business formats that are not valuable) have an incentive to claim that they are offering a valuable business format. Claims of format value, if believed by potential franchisees, will result in sales of outlets.

Given the ineffectiveness of just "claiming" value as a way to persuade potential franchisees to partner with them, you need to take strategic actions to show prospective franchisees that your system is, indeed, valuable. You can do this by taking an observable stake in its profitability. By owning and operating units, your profits become directly dependent on the value of the business format. Because only franchisors with valuable business formats are willing to invest in them, this willingness to invest provides persuasive evidence that franchisees should buy into the system.

As a result, franchisee advisors strongly urge potential franchisees not to believe new franchisors' claims about the value of business formats, but to "investigate before they invest" and invest in only those in which the value of the system is clearly demonstrated. Specifically, franchisee advisors tell prospective franchisees to buy only franchises in which franchisors operate some of their own outlets. For instance, Rob Bond, the publisher of *Sourcebook of Franchise Opportunities*, a popular guide to franchising, explains, "the mix of company-owned vs. franchised units is indicative of the willingness of the franchisor to 'put his money where his mouth is' to some extent."[3]

Similarly, in her own advice book to franchisees, franchise consultant Bev Cline writes,

> The first question [that interested franchisees should ask about any new system] is whether the principals of the new system have an equity interest in the operation. The franchisor should own at least one or two company stores so that he has a real stake in the continuity of the system. If the franchisor tells you that his sole role is in selling units, my advice would be to run in the opposite direction.[4]

As a new franchisor, the more outlets that you own, the more your performance depends on the value of your business format. Therefore, the more company-owned outlets you have, the greater the signal is to franchisees that you will invest in upholding the value of the system.

The Early Growth Period

In their early years, most successful franchisors keep stable the number of company-owned outlets that they have and add franchised outlets almost exclusively. By doing this, successful franchisors drive down the proportion of company-owned outlets in their systems in the early growth period.

Successful franchisors adopt this strategy for a few reasons. First, most franchisors would like to franchise the new outlets that they add because of the many benefits of franchising described in Chapter 2, "The Advantages of Franchising." Moreover, franchisees are attracted by the opportunity to obtain the best outlets, which they cannot do unless the franchisor franchises them.

During this growth period, the need to own a lot of outlets to signal the value of the franchise system declines because successful franchisors develop reputations for having valuable systems. Prospective franchisees can look at the performance of the company-owned outlets and the first outlets franchised. Combined with the opportunity to examine the product or service, this evaluation allows them to determine the value of buying into the system without requiring the franchisor to own additional outlets.

In the early growth period, successful franchisors do not sell off the company-owned outlets that they had established previously. Even when the signaling benefit of owning outlets is no longer important, successful franchisors still see value in operating some of their own outlets directly. Company-owned outlets serve as an R&D laboratory, where franchisors can improve the products and services offered to customers, identify the most effective outlet operations, and develop the right policies to monitor and provide incentives to franchisees. These outlets also provide a place to train potential franchisees and field operation personnel in the business system.

Buying Back Outlets in Mature Systems

As successful franchisors mature, they tend to buy back outlets, increasing their share of company-owned outlets.[5] One reason for this is that the profits from operating outlets are higher than from franchising them, leading successful franchisors to repurchase their most profitable outlets. For instance, both McDonald's and Taco Bell® aggressively bought back their highest performing outlets when their systems reached maturity. This effort to buy back outlets as a way to earn higher profits is particularly common when franchisors believe that they can increase sales or reduce costs through the centralization of operations.

In addition, as franchisors become mature, the financial resource constraints that they face decline, making greater outlet ownership more viable. Many mature franchisors go public or obtain significant infusions of capital, reducing the need for franchising as a way to access capital. As a result, mature franchisors take advantage of their greater access to capital to repurchase profitable outlets.

At the same time that they are experiencing reduced constraints to owning outlets, most mature franchisors experience strong incentives to own outlets to minimize conflict with franchisees. When franchisors grow large, they tend to saturate their markets, making it more difficult to sell additional franchises. The saturation of markets makes franchises less attractive to franchisees, who see lower profits from buying a franchise in the system than when markets were less densely populated with outlets. Once system growth slows, franchisors also have less incentive to uphold their agreements to provide advertising and support services to franchisees. The combination of these factors leads to conflict between franchisors and franchisees that could potentially result in litigation. By buying back outlets, franchisors can minimize the potential for litigation with franchisees.

Conversion Franchising

The patterns just described are true for most types of franchising, with one exception: conversion franchises. Conversion franchising is a process by which existing independent businesses are brought under the franchisor's umbrella. A good example of a conversion franchisor is Century 21® Real Estate, out of Parsippany, New Jersey.[6] Because conversion franchisors bring a large number of independent businesses under the franchisor's umbrella rather than selling franchises to people seeking to start businesses, many of the arguments about the value of company-owned outlets do not apply to conversion franchises.

Conversion franchising has its own pros and cons. On the positive side, it increases the likelihood that franchisees have relevant business experience. Conversion franchises tend to know how to run outlets in their industries because they typically have been doing so for many years before converting to the franchise chain. In addition, conversion franchising offers benefits of the outlet's operating history for the performance of the outlet. Because many retail operations experience a learning curve at the outlet level, the performance of conversion franchises tends to be high shortly after franchising begins. Furthermore, conversion franchising can create a large chain very quickly, allowing the franchisor to take advantage of economies of scale in advertising and purchasing.

On the negative side, conversion franchising requires the franchisor to incorporate an independent businessperson used to doing things his or her own way into an operating system.[7] As will be discussed in greater detail in Chapter 11, "Recruiting, Selecting, and Managing Franchisees," many franchisors do not like to franchise to experienced entrepreneurs. Their desire for independence conflicts with the need for standardization in the franchise system and can often lead to poor performance.

Stop! Don't Do It!

1. Don't franchise without owning some of your own outlets.
2. Don't be afraid to buy back outlets when your franchise system becomes mature; it is often the best strategy once markets become saturated.

Which Outlets to Franchise

To be successful at franchising, you should franchise geographically distant outlets and own those near your headquarters. Outlets farther from headquarters are more expensive to monitor because of the cost of sending field auditors to the franchisee's location. Therefore, using a mechanism such as franchising that requires less monitoring is more effective in more distant locations.

You should also franchise outlets that you establish in rural areas and own those that you locate in urban or suburban areas that are densely populated. In densely populated areas, you can establish more outlets per square mile, allowing you to get economies of scale in monitoring from your district managers. This lowers your cost of monitoring and makes it cost-effective to supervise outlets directly rather than franchising them. In addition, the value of your outlet managers to sales generation is lower than the value of your district managers when there are multiple outlets in an area and the promotion activities are coordinated by district mangers. Therefore, the advertising and promotional benefits of company ownership are greater in densely populated areas.

You should also own outlets in locations where repeat customers are less frequent, such as tourist areas. Free riding (as described in Chapter 3, "The Disadvantages of Franchising") is a major problem with franchising; but company-owned outlet managers do not have an incentive to free-ride. Therefore, you want to own outlets in locations where free riding is a major risk that could undermine outlet performance. Because reputation effects are an alternative to ownership for controlling free riding, franchisors often use company ownership when reputation effects are limited. Reputation effects are limited in locations where repeat customers are rare, so franchising is less effective in those locations.

For example, Baskin-Robbins® will want to own its ice cream shops in beach resorts because franchisees in those locations will be more likely to get away with free riding on the company's reputation by providing skimpy portions for the same price and pocketing the difference. In nontourist areas, repeat customers would provide a mechanism to keep franchisee portion size in line: They won't come back if franchisees are skimping on the size of ice cream cones. But in tourist areas, with most customers being one-time patrons, the reputation mechanism doesn't work to control franchisee free riding, leading franchisors to own the outlets and avoid this problem.

You should own outlets in which performance is not highly correlated with other outlets in your system or that have very variable performance. Under those circumstances, it is easier for franchisees to engage in opportunistic behavior because you will not be able to evaluate them by comparing their performance to system norms. Therefore, monitoring those outlets directly is important to efforts to control what happens at the outlet.[8]

For example, a fast food chain such as Arby's® will want to own the first few restaurants it sets up in novel locations such as airports or college campuses. These outlets are likely to differ greatly in terms of hours, costs, sales, and other dimensions that franchisors rely on to measure the performance of franchisees. Until Arby's has a large enough number of outlets in airports and college campuses to compare the performance of those outlets to each other, it will have difficulty detecting whether franchisee poor performance is a result of opportunistic action. As a result, it is better off owning the outlets to ensure that this problem cannot occur.

Stop! Don't Do It!

1. Don't own your outlets far away from headquarters or in densely populated areas.
2. Don't franchise outlets in locations with few repeat customers.

Geographic Expansion Strategy

As a franchisor, you need to determine what geographic expansion strategy your franchise system will adopt. As mentioned earlier, franchising tends to occur in businesses in which revenue growth comes from establishing additional locations rather than from expanding the operations at existing locations. This means that the approach you adopt to adding locations in new geographic areas has an important influence on the performance of your company.

Although many new franchisors adopt a shotgun approach, establishing franchises anywhere someone is willing to buy them, successful franchisors tend to expand in a geographically constrained manner, concentrating their new units in only one or two states until they have reached a large enough scale to expand to other areas. For example, Arabica Coffee House, a successful coffee shop franchise with 47 units, operates only in the state of Ohio.[9]

Geographic concentration of outlets is a good strategy for you to follow when you set up a franchise system because it facilitates quality control. Shotgun-style expansion makes quality control difficult because it raises the cost of sending franchise consultants to audit franchisees and leads you to underinvest in monitoring your franchisees. For instance, a new print shop franchise that establishes its first five outlets in New York, San Francisco, Los Angeles, Chicago, and Miami will find that it is much more expensive to send its franchise consultants to those outlets to monitor them than a new print shop franchise that establishes its first five outlets within the five boroughs of New York City. As a result, given a fixed amount of money available for monitoring franchisees, the first franchisor is likely to have weaker control over its franchisees than the second franchisor.

In addition, shotgun expansion provides franchisees with an incentive to engage in problematic activity while franchise consultants are away from their territories and unable to check on them. Furthermore, a lack of geographically concentrated expansion makes it hard to achieve economies of scale in key activities to spur growth, such as advertising. Because most advertising markets are local, you can run radio and print advertisements more cost effectively if you operate several outlets in media markets. For instance, by concentrating its franchisees in specific geographic locations, Tastee-Freez was able to create local advertising pools, allowing the company to advertise more cost effectively than more geographically dispersed franchise systems with which it competed.[10]

Stop! Don't Do It!

1. Don't adopt a shotgun approach to your initial franchising efforts; concentrate your outlets in a few media markets.

International Expansion

If you are successful at franchising, eventually you will be confronted with the issue of international expansion, if for no other reason than the fact that franchising has become an international activity. Approximately 400 U.S. franchisors now operate more than 30,000 outlets outside of the United States.

Of course, the days when franchising was purely an American export are over. Now when franchisors expand overseas, they must compete with not only local businesses in their industry, but also local franchisors. For example, in Columbia, the Oma chain of franchised cafes has grown from a few outlets to more than 50 outlets in five years.[11] Consequently, foreign coffee house franchisors seeking to enter the Columbia market face a formidable competitor in the local market.

Moreover, franchising has become a global business. Even back in the United States, coffee house franchisors now face competition from competitors from Columbia. The National Federation of Coffee Growers from Columbia is currently expanding into the

United States with 2 franchised locations to add to its base of 11 Columbian cafes.[12] As a result, American coffee house franchisors such as Gloria Jean's and Seattle's Best Coffee have to compete with foreign franchising competition, as well as American franchisors and nonfranchisors, such as Starbucks.

As a franchisor, you are faced with two key questions about international activity: When should you expand overseas? And when you do, what changes do you need to make to your franchise operations? The following sections offer some answers to those questions.

When to Expand Overseas

To expand overseas successfully, your franchise system needs to have reached a reasonable level of maturity. When you first begin to franchise, international operations will be very difficult, if not impossible, for you to manage. Initially, you will need to tweak your business model, so having franchisees near your headquarters is important so that they can make rapid adjustments to their operations as they receive feedback from you about such things as training, site selection, sourcing of supplies, and advertising. Moreover, locations in foreign countries are difficult to monitor not only because gathering information on locations far away from headquarters is difficult and costly, but also because of the uncertainties of the international business environment that come from differences in cultures, exchange rates, and economies.

Several years of operating your franchise system in your home market will facilitate later international expansion because it will provide you with knowledge of how to manage your system effectively, as well as how to identify the right franchisees to sell to and the right locations to select. Your experience as a franchisor will also help you to figure out how to transfer your operating system to foreign franchisees, which is much more difficult to accomplish than transferring the same system to domestic franchisees.

More important, several years of domestic operations will lead you to engage in international operations because longevity makes it more likely that you will have saturated your home market, an important trigger of overseas expansion. Market saturation leads to international expansion because it leads to shrinking profit margins as you try to find domestic franchisees in an increasingly limited domestic market.

Even after they have saturated their home markets, most franchisors do not expand overseas until they receive the right trigger, which is typically an inquiry from someone overseas interested in buying into the system. In fact, almost two-thirds of U.S. franchisors expand overseas in response to an inquiry from someone in another country. This pattern indicates that most franchisors do not expand overseas as part of a concerted foreign expansion strategy. Rather, they tend to fall into this activity after they have become fairly large domestic franchisors.

In fact, a study by Arthur Andersen showed that the average U.S. franchisor had 137 domestic outlets when it set up its first overseas outlet.[13] Although there is some variation in this number across industries and between franchisors within industries, the large average size indicates that most first-time international franchisors are not new, small franchisors, but are relatively large, mature systems.

Changes You Need to Make for International Expansion

To be successful in your international expansion, you need to alter your policies and strategies. Like most franchisors, you probably want to use master franchising rather than direct franchising to enter overseas markets.[14] Master franchising helps you with your efforts to move into foreign markets because it dramatically reduces the costly and inefficient process of managing a large number of individual franchisees at a distance. It also removes the burden of understanding how to operate in another country, something that most franchisors are ill-equipped to do. By partnering with a master franchisee, you can use that company's local market expertise to facilitate the adaptation of the system and monitoring mechanisms to the new market. It also makes it easier for you to select the right foreign franchisees, which is very costly to do internationally.

However, the use of master franchising internationally is not free of costs or risks. Master franchisees do not always uphold system standards, and you have to be ready to terminate your foreign master franchisees if they fail to perform. McDonald's, for example, had to terminate its initial master franchisee in France when it discovered that the franchisee was not adhering to cleanliness standards and found rodents in the restaurants.[15]

You should make several other changes when you expand overseas. You should charge higher up-front fees and lower ongoing royalties when you sell franchises to foreign franchisees. Your ability to monitor franchisees at a distance, combined with differences in legal environments, make it harder to enforce franchise agreements, trademark rights, and noncompete clauses internationally. As a result, you should take more of your compensation up front when expanding to foreign markets.

You should also train your foreign franchisees differently than your domestic franchisees. Half of all franchisors change the content of their training when expanding overseas. In general, they make the training more appropriate to the local market and adjust the form of the training to minimize costs. In particular, to keep costs down, successful franchisors generally require their foreign franchisees to come to their U.S. headquarters for training rather than provide training at the franchisee's site. As a result, significantly fewer franchisors offer on-the-job training to non-U.S. franchisees than they do to U.S. franchisees.[16]

In general, when you expand overseas, you should also rely more heavily on franchised outlets than you do in your home market, although this reliance on franchising should decline as your company becomes more experienced at international operations.[17] The exact degree to which you should rely on franchising when you expand your system overseas depends on a variety of factors, such as the characteristics of the target market. For instance, you should franchise more heavily in countries that are economically or politically riskier because franchising is an effective tool for shedding risk onto franchisees.

You should also franchise more of your overseas outlets the more culturally different your target market is from the United States. In culturally different markets, you should take advantage of the local market expertise of franchisees in adapting your product or service to their markets. Monitoring is also more costly to undertake internationally than domestically and is harder to do correctly the more different the country is from the United States. By franchising, you can reduce the level of monitoring required, making franchising more important with overseas outlets than with domestic ones.[18]

On the other hand, you should be less reliant on franchising your overseas outlets if you have made a large investment in the development of your company's brand name. Your franchise system is just as vulnerable to the problems of free riding on brand names that were discussed in Chapter 3 when you operate internationally as when you operate domestically. However, the cost of monitoring your franchisees against this free riding is greater internationally because the cost of monitoring increases as the cultural and physical distance between you and your franchisees grows. As was explained earlier, companies often own their outlets as a way to control free riding because managers of company-owned outlets do not have the same incentive to free-ride as franchisees. Therefore, if you have made a large investment in the development of your company's brand name, you should own more outlets when your system expands overseas.[19]

Stop! Don't Do It!

1. Don't expand overseas until your business is older and larger, and has saturated your domestic market.

2. Don't expand overseas with exactly the same strategy that you used in your home market; success at overseas expansion requires changes to system policies.

Questions to Ask Yourself

1. When should I begin franchising?
2. How many outlets should I own?
3. Which outlets should I franchise?
4. How should I expand my operations geographically?
5. When should I expand my system overseas?
6. What changes should I make to my system for foreign operations?

Summary

This chapter discussed the components of a successful franchise-expansion strategy. Because franchising tends to occur in businesses for which expansion can't occur at one location, but instead requires the addition of new outlets, the magnitude of profits that you earn from franchising depends largely on how quickly and effectively you expand the number of locations where you serve customers. A successful expansion strategy will increase your business's profits, whereas a poor expansion plan will undermine the performance of your operation.

The first dimension of a successful franchise-expansion strategy lies in figuring out when in your company's life to begin franchising. The right time is usually several years after initiating company operations, when the kinks in your operating system have been worked out. However, the right time varies by industry, and you need to make sure that your timing fits your industry.

The second dimension of a successful franchise-expansion strategy involves determining the right number of outlets to own. Although most franchisors franchise about four-fifths of their outlets, the proportion of franchised outlets in franchise chains varies significantly over the life of a franchise system. When you first begin to franchise, you need to operate some of your own outlets because outlet ownership provides a credible signal of the value of your system to franchisees. In growth years of franchising, you will want to keep your number of company-owned outlets stable and franchise new outlets almost exclusively. This approach will allow you to take advantage of the benefits of franchising to the growth of your system. However, you will want to maintain some company-owned outlets because these outlets provide a useful R&D laboratory for developing new products and services, and figuring out how to manage franchisees, as well as a place to train potential franchisees and field operations personnel.

When your system matures, you should buy back some outlets because ownership is more profitable than franchising. Your ability to adopt this more profitable approach becomes possible after resource constraints on the growth of your business have been reduced. In addition, your growth will lead to market saturation and conflict with franchisees, which can be mitigated by repurchasing their outlets.

You should franchise the outlets in your chain that are geographically the most distant from headquarters and ones in less densely populated areas because these outlets are the most expensive for you to monitor. In contrast, you should own outlets where there are few repeat customers and where performance is not highly correlated with the performance of other outlets in the system.

When you first begin franchising, concentrating your outlets geographically is a good strategy to follow because it facilitates monitoring franchisees and maintaining quality control. Geographic concentration also facilitates the development of economies of scale in local advertising, which reduces the cost of building your brand name.

If you are successful, you will be confronted eventually with the issue of international competition, whether that competition comes from expanding overseas or from foreign franchisors entering your home market. You should expand overseas when your business has reached a reasonable level of maturity, having franchised for several years and thus having created a relatively large chain that has saturated your domestic market.

When you expand overseas, you are better off using master franchising than franchising directly. You also should charge higher up-front fees and lower ongoing royalties. Concentrating your franchisee training at your headquarters is a good idea, given the cost of overseas travel. You also want to rely more heavily on franchising than you do in your home market, particularly if your target markets are culturally distant from the United States. However, if you have made large investments in the development of your brand name, you probably want to own more of your outlets, to minimize the problems of franchisee free riding.

Now that you understand the key components of a successful franchise-expansion strategy, we turn to the legal and institutional context of franchising in the next chapter.

10

THE LEGAL AND INSTITUTIONAL ENVIRONMENT FOR FRANCHISING

Franchising is a legally regulated mode of doing business. This means that, to be successful, you need to understand the effects of federal and state franchise laws on the operation of your franchise system. You might have the best business concept in the world, but you will not attract franchisees, operate effectively, or make money if your franchise system does not conform to federal and state regulatory requirements.

This chapter offers specific information to make sure that you understand the key legal issues in franchising. Specifically, the chapter discusses the key federal and state franchise regulations and explains how they affect franchise operations. The chapter examines the pros and cons of expanding in franchise registration states, focusing on the trade-offs involved in disclosing litigation and bankruptcy history, providing audited financial statements, and meeting bonding requirements, all of which are necessary to meet registration requirements. It also considers the benefits and costs of operating in states with franchise-termination laws.

The chapter also discusses the role of certification in franchising. Specifically, it considers the benefits of membership in the International Franchise Association, the industry trade association, and certification by the media.

Federal Law

Since 1979, the United States Federal Trade Commission (FTC) has required all franchisors to furnish prospective franchisees with information about the company franchising and its principals in an offering circular document at least 10 days before the signing of a franchise agreement. Although the FTC now exempts franchisors who sell franchises only overseas and sales to those franchisees deemed "sophisticated" from this disclosure requirement, this requirement means that franchisors must provide their primary potential franchisees with a standard document about their business prior to selling them a franchise.

To meet federal requirements, franchisors can use the FTC version of the standard offering circular or a Uniform Franchise Offering Circular (UFOC). This latter document, first created by the Midwest Securities Commissioners Association in 1975, is the form preferred by most registration states.[1] The preference of state regulators for the UFOC means that most franchisors seeking to sell franchises in registration states opt to use this document.

The UFOC is a standard document; all franchisors must provide the same 23 items of information. Table 10.1 lists the items that franchisors are required to disclose to potential franchisees in their UFOCs.

TABLE 10.1   Items Required for Disclosure in a UFOC

1. The franchisor and predecessors
2. Business experience of persons affiliated with the franchisor
3. Litigation history
4. Bankruptcy history
5. Initial fee
6. Other fees
7. Initial investment
8. Restrictions of franchisee sourcing
9. Franchisee's obligations
10. Financing
11. Franchisor's obligations
12. Territory
13. Trademarks and service marks
14. Patents and copyrights
15. Obligation of the franchisee to participate in the business
16. Restrictions on franchisee sale of goods and services
17. Renewal and termination
18. Arrangements with public figures
19. Earnings claims
20. Statistics on system
21. Audited financial statements
22. Contracts
23. Acknowledgment of receipt

The requirement that you create a UFOC is one of the things that makes starting to franchise costly. To create the UFOC, you need to hire an experienced franchise attorney—and they do not come cheaply. Moreover, one of the items required in a UFOC is an audited financial statement. Because audited financials are much more expensive than unaudited ones, your accounting expenses go up significantly when you begin to franchise. Furthermore, if you make claims about franchisee earnings from ownership of your outlets, you need to provide an additional disclosure about those earnings.

Stop! Don't Do It!

1. Don't sell franchises without first offering franchisees a disclosure document; you will be in violation of federal law.

2. Don't get creative with franchise offering circulars; you need to include all of the standard items.

State Law

Franchisors face two broad categories of state laws. The first consists of laws regarding what franchisors can and cannot do to sell franchises, and it involves requirements for registration and dissemination of information. The second consists of state laws governing relationships between franchisors and franchisees, and it governs such issues as franchisee termination.

Not all states have franchise regulations; states with registration laws might or might not have relationship laws. The variance across the states in the legal environment for franchising makes understanding which states have which laws important in developing your franchise system strategy and policies. Table 10.2 lists the states with registration and relationship laws.

TABLE 10.2   States with Registration and Relationship Laws

States with Registration Laws	States with Relationship Laws
California	Arkansas
Hawaii	California
Illinois	Connecticut
Indiana	Delaware
Maryland	Florida
Michigan	Hawaii
Minnesota	Illinois
New York	Indiana
North Dakota	Iowa
Oregon	Kentucky
Rhode Island	Maryland
South Dakota	Michigan
Virginia	Minnesota
Washington	Mississippi
Wisconsin	Missouri
	Nebraska
	New Jersey
	North Dakota
	South Dakota
	Virginia
	Washington
	Wisconsin

Registration States

Registration laws are laws that require franchisors who want to sell franchises in a state to provide a copy of their UFOC to the regulatory authorities before they begin to sell franchises in the state. (A franchisor can provide a franchisee with the FTC version except in California, Indiana, Maryland, Minnesota, Rhode Island, South Dakota, Virginia, and Washington, where only the UFOC version is acceptable.) These laws also require franchisors to file reports with state regulators at least annually, and in some of the states, quarterly.

Since 2000, franchisors have been able to register their systems with all registration state authorities simultaneously and might soon be allowed to send disclosure documents to franchisees in electronic form.

The registration requirement has several effects on franchising. First and foremost, it provides an additional level of scrutiny of the information that franchisors provide to franchisees, which makes it more likely that franchisees operating in registration states provide their franchisees with accurate information about the system.

In addition, it provides some modicum of protection of franchisee investment in the franchise system. In most of the registration states, the regulatory authorities require you, the franchisor, to put any fees paid by your franchisees into escrow until you have provided the services that the fees are to cover, if the state regulators do not believe that your company's financial condition is strong enough to ensure provision of those services. In other registration states, you are required to post a bond to guarantee that franchise fees are used for the opening of outlets if regulators judge your balance sheet to be weak. Regulators in these states often see it as too risky for franchisees to purchase from an undercapitalized franchisor (with the definition of undercapitalized being a franchisor whose net worth is less than the franchisee's initial investment).[2]

The regulatory authorities in many registration states also must approve any advertisements made by you, the franchisor, to attract franchisees. Typically, the state regulators want to ensure that you don't make any statements about expected performance and success of your franchisees in your advertisements.

If you are a franchisor in a registration state, you are required to update your offering circular on record with the state authorities whenever you make a "material change" to your franchise system. A material change is any change to the fees charged to franchisees, their obligations, the operating system, the legal structure of the franchisor, financial information, or a program for interacting with franchisees.[3] Not only does the material change notification requirement impose a compliance burden on your company, but it also makes it difficult for you, as a franchisor, to negotiate with franchisees over your franchise agreement because of the required notification of any changes negotiated with franchisees.[4] (You should also try to minimize differences in the contracts given to different franchisees because they could cause your system to run afoul of state antidiscrimination laws.[5])

The registration requirements imposed by some states and not others lead to an important set of regulatory strategy choices. As a franchisor, you can choose not to operate in registration states, as a way to avoid this regulatory burden. In fact, about half of all franchisors do just that. In 1998, there were 1,398 registered franchise systems, approximately one half of all franchisors selling franchises at that point in time.[6]

Because many states in the Southeast and Southwest do not require registration, you can adopt a regional expansion strategy by focusing on the nonregistration states. Only after you have saturated the market in nonregistration states do you need to incur the additional cost and burden of moving into registration states. For example, Arthur Treacher's Fish and Chips operates 203 franchised outlets in 21 states but is registered in only 3 of the 16 registration states.[7]

On the other hand, you might want to operate your new franchise in registration states as a way to signal its quality to franchisees. The oversight that comes from regulators helps to weed out bad franchises. Only franchisors that know that they are operating legitimate and valuable businesses are willing to submit to this extra oversight. As a result, franchisors that operate in registration states have an easier time attracting franchisees than those that do not. In fact, research has shown that successful new franchisors are 22 percent more likely than unsuccessful franchisors to operate in a registration state.[8]

Moreover, the benefits of operating in registration states increase with system size. The cost of operating in registration states drops as system size increases because large franchisors are often exempt from many registration requirements. Moreover, the cost of not operating in registration states increases as system size goes up: Large systems that do not operate in registration states give the impression that they have something to hide and are avoiding registration states, while small systems can explain that approach simply as part of their expansion strategies.

Relationship States

States also differ on whether they have franchise relationship laws, or laws that govern the interaction between franchisors and franchisees. These laws are designed to protect franchisees by making sure that franchisors have "good cause" to terminate franchisees and by giving franchisees the right to cure contract violations. Good cause generally means that the franchisor can terminate the contract if the franchisee has engaged in some type of breach of contract.[9] Table 10.3 shows the states with different franchise relationship provisions.

TABLE 10.3   States with Different Relationship Provisions

States That Require Cause for Termination	States That Allow Cure in Termination
Arkansas	Arkansas
California	California
Connecticut	Hawaii
Delaware	Illinois
Hawaii	Michigan
Illinois	Minnesota
Indiana	Washington
Michigan	Wisconsin
Minnesota	
Nebraska	
New Jersey	
Virginia	
Washington	
Wisconsin	

Franchise relationship laws have several important implications for the management of franchise systems. By requiring "good cause" for termination, franchise relationship laws raise the standard that you, the franchisor, need to meet for not renewing your franchisees. As a result, if you operate your franchise system in states with relationship laws, you face higher costs to terminating your franchisees.

These additional costs lead franchisors in relationship law states to raise royalty rates above what they are in other states. Jim Brickley, a professor at the University of Rochester, has shown that franchisors headquartered in states with franchise termination laws charge royalty rates of roughly 1 percent more than other franchisors, but franchise fees of roughly $4,000 less.[10]

Franchise relationship laws also make it easier for you to attract franchisees to your franchise system. By protecting franchisees, relationship laws make people more willing to buy franchises in relationship law states than they are in other states. This makes a heavier reliance on franchising an effective strategy in those states. In fact, research shows that new franchisors headquartered in termination states that make more extensive use of franchised outlets are less likely than other new franchisors to fail.[11]

However, franchise relationship laws also make the threat of termination a less effective method of policing quality than otherwise is the case. These states have greater problems with franchisee free riding, making them less popular in industries with fewer repeat customers. Although repeat customers provide a reputation effect that deters free riding, those industries that lack repeat customers have no good mechanism to deter free riding when the threat of termination is weakened. As a result, firms are less likely to engage in franchising in relationship states in businesses with few repeat customers.[12]

Stop! Don't Do It!

1. Don't try to sell franchises in registration states if your business is undercapitalized.
2. Don't rely on the threat of termination to keep franchisees in line in relationship states; "good cause" and "right to cure" provisions will make it difficult to enforce your threat.

Franchisor Certification

Another important institutional issue that you want to think about when you establish your franchise system is certification by key actors. Winning contests for your products or services, or getting your franchise system ranked by magazines and newspapers is something that you want to achieve. Research has shown that the performance of franchise systems is enhanced by certification by reputable authorities. The media is a particularly important source of certification for firms because magazines and newspapers provide information on what businesses are legitimate and desirable partners. For instance, franchise systems that are ranked highly in *Entrepreneur Magazine*'s Franchise 500® are more likely than other franchise systems to survive over time.

Membership in the industry trade association, the International Franchise Association (IFA), also serves an important certification function. Because the IFA is made up of only 600 of the approximately 2,500 franchisors in existence at any point in time, and its members tend to be the oldest and largest franchisors, you can signal the quality of your franchise system by joining the IFA. Membership in the IFA requires you to adhere to standards that are higher than the average for the franchising market. You must certify that you have never been "convicted of a felony or been held liable in a civil action involving fraud, fraudulent conversion, or misappropriation of property."[13] In addition, you cannot be:

[S]ubject to any order of the Securities and Exchange Commission or the securities administrator of any state denying, revoking, or suspending the registration or sale of any securities property...subject to any order or ruling of the Federal Trade Commission property...[or] subject to any injunctive or restrictive order relating to business activity as a result of any action brought by any public agency or department property.... [Nor can the franchisor be] subject to any order issued under any federal or state law regulating the sale of franchises or distributorships which denies, revokes, or suspends the registration or sale of franchises or distributorships within any jurisdiction or requires the posting of a bond, the escrow of monies to be paid by franchisees or distributorships, or any similar action [as] a precondition of the registration or sale of franchises or distributorships property.[14]

Moreover, you must certify that you have read and will comply with the International Franchise Association code of conduct. This certification is a particularly important signal because the cost of failing to adhere to this code of conduct is high for franchisors. Franchise attorney Rupert Barkoff has explained that "there is concern among franchisor's counsel that in litigation the [IFA] code will be introduced as evidence of a standard which, if not complied with, may result in liability to the franchisor for, among other reasons, breach of an implied covenant of good faith and fair dealing."[15]

Thus, it is not surprising that research has shown that franchisors who are members of the IFA perform better than those who are not members. In a study of 157 new franchisors that I conducted for the Office of Advocacy of the U.S. Small Business Administration, I found that new franchisors who became members of the IFA were 11 percent more likely to survive over time than other new franchise systems.[16]

The value of IFA membership increases with franchise system size. One reason for this is that membership has a fixed cost component. As a result, the cost of membership drops on a per-outlet basis as the system increases in size. Moreover, large systems suffer more from not joining the IFA than small systems. Small organizations might argue that the cost of membership deters them from joining, but large organizations that do not join are perceived as having something to hide.

Stop! Don't Do It!

1. Don't forget to seek certification from reputable authorities; it enhances system performance.
2. Don't avoid membership in the IFA, especially as your system grows; the trade association provides an important certification function.

Questions to Ask Yourself

1. Do I have a management team that understands the legal aspects of franchising?
2. Am I willing to incur the legal costs of setting up a franchise operation?
3. Am I willing to disclose past litigation and bankruptcy history and provide audited financial statements to franchisees?
4. Am I willing to provide a bond or escrow to state regulatory authorities?
5. Do I have a plan for obtaining certification for my franchise system?

Summary

Franchising is a legally regulated mode of doing business. This chapter discussed the federal and state laws that affect the operation of franchise systems. You need to conform to these laws if you are going to make your franchise system successful.

Since 1979, the Federal Trade Commission has required all franchisors to furnish prospective franchisees with information about the franchise and its principals in an offering circular prior to the signing of a franchise agreement. The standard disclosure document, the Uniform Franchise Offering Circular, includes 23 items that you, the franchisor, must disclose. In addition, if you provide earnings claims to prospective franchises, you must provide additional disclosure documents.

Franchisors face two broad categories of state laws. The first category consists of registration laws, which govern what you can and cannot do to sell your franchise. Registration laws require franchisors who want to sell franchises to provide a copy of their UFOC to regulatory authorities before they begin to sell franchises in the state, and to update their UFOCs at least annually or when they have made a material change to their systems. In registration states, regulatory authorities require franchisors to post a bond before they are allowed to collect franchise fees if they have a weak balance sheet. These authorities must also approve any ads used to attract franchisees.

Only some states have laws governing franchising, leading to an interesting strategic choice. You can operate only in nonregistration states when your franchise system is young and small as a way to save costs, or you can choose to operate in registration states to signal your system's quality.

The second category of state laws governs relationships between franchisors and franchisees. These laws are designed to make sure that you have good cause to terminate your franchisees, and that your franchisees have the right to cure contract violations. Relationship laws raise the cost of franchisee termination, leading franchisors to charge higher royalty rates and lower up-front fees, but these franchisors have an easier time attracting franchisees when operating in a relationship state.

A final legal and institutional issue that you, as a franchisor, will want to consider is the certification of your franchise system by key actors. Research has shown that certification by the media or by trade association membership enhances franchisor performance.

Now that you understand the key legal and institutional issues in franchising, you can delve into the issues of recruiting, selecting, and managing franchisees; these are the subject of the next chapter.

11

RECRUITING, SELECTING, AND MANAGING FRANCHISEES

When you start to franchise, you enter a new business. You are in the business of franchising, not in the business of serving customers in the industry in which your franchisees provide a product or service. As a result, your success depends largely on your ability to recruit, select, and manage franchisees.

This chapter offers specific information to help you to determine how to recruit, select, and manage the franchisees who will deliver your product or service to customers using your business system. The first part of this chapter discusses how to recruit franchisees. Offering information on what franchisees look for in a franchise system and how they select one system over another, this section helps you to formulate a recruiting strategy for your system. To be successful, you also need to sell talented franchisees on the opportunity to buy a business opportunity. Therefore, this section also discusses ways to create a solid pool of potential franchisees and an effective sales force to convert that pool into actual franchisees.

Contrary to popular opinion and the pronouncements of the franchise trade association, the average franchisee has worse performance than the average independent business owner. But this is not because franchising does not provide a lot of value to franchisees. Rather, it is because the average franchisee is not as good at operating a business as the average independent business owner. This, of course, means that you need to screen potential franchisees carefully to pick the successful ones. The second section of the chapter offers a template for selecting motivated and skilled franchisees.

The third section discusses how to manage your franchisees effectively. In general, effective franchisee management has four components:

- Making sure that participation in your system generates financial benefit for your franchisees

- Minimizing the number of issues on which you and your franchisees have goal conflict

- Specifying the rules of the franchise system clearly in your franchise contract and communicating them clearly to your franchisees

- Monitoring your franchisees carefully and enforcing the rules of the franchise system

If you do these four things, your franchisees will respect you, work with you, and generate financial returns for both you and them.

Recruiting Franchisees

To be successful as a franchisor, you need to recruit franchisees. Performance at this activity is largely about two things: understanding why people buy franchises, and offering them something that they want to buy; and developing a professional franchise sales force that knows how to generate a pool of prospects and sell them on your franchise system.

Why Do People Buy Franchises?

People buy franchises to get access to a proven system and to make money.[1] Therefore, to recruit franchisees, you need to make sure that your franchise system provides these two benefits—and does so better than other alternatives available to prospective franchisees. You also need to keep in mind that, when selling franchises, your competition is not only franchisors offering businesses in your same industry. Rather, it is franchisors operating in a wide variety of industries. For example, when potential franchisees go to a franchise trade show looking for opportunities to buy, they might very well see Speedy Transmission Center® and Dunkin Donuts franchises as substitutes, even though end users aren't going to get their cars repaired instead of buying donuts. Prospective franchisees often look across a wide range of industries for franchise opportunities, expressing relatively little concern for the product or service it actually provides. After all, the franchisor that they buy from is going to provide them with the knowledge that it takes to be successful in whatever business they end up pursuing.

The first thing that you need to do to recruit franchisees is offer a valuable operating system. Much of what you need to do to ensure that you have a valuable business format was covered in Chapter 4, "What Business Concepts Can Be Franchised?" (You might want to look at that chapter again). But the key points can be summarized here briefly. The system has to work. The bugs in the operation of serving end customers need to have been worked out, and the system needs to have been shown to be successful in a company-owned outlet.

The franchise needs to come with a manual that explains how to operate the business—and you, the franchisor, need to provide initial training and assistance in opening the outlet and ongoing operations.

You, as a franchisor, also need to offer a way to centralize certain activities that are subject to economies of scale, such as purchasing or advertising. Finally, your franchise system needs to offer a brand name that attracts customers.

The second thing that you need to do to attract franchisees is offer them an opportunity to make a very good profit. For example, McDonald's generates a profit stream for its franchisees that significantly exceeds what they could be earning at alternative employment. As a result, there is a long line of people who want to become McDonald's franchisees, making recruiting franchisees very easy for McDonald's.[2]

Whereas people might know that McDonald's franchises are profitable through word-of-mouth, you might need to provide some evidence to potential franchisees that they can make money by purchasing an outlet in your system. How do you show franchisees that they have an opportunity to make a good profit by operating one of your outlets? Obviously, you need some sort of business opportunity that is profitable at the outlet level. If you are operating a business and making money at the outlet level, there is a good chance that you have a business in which franchisees can make money.

However, you can't just claim that your business is profitable to franchisees; that's illegal. If you want to tell potential franchisees that they will make good money operating a franchise in your system, you need to provide them with an earnings claim disclosure.

Earnings claims are any information that that the franchisor gives to a potential franchisee that indicates a level of sales or earnings that will come from purchasing a franchise. The Federal Trade Commission officially defines an earnings claim as "any oral, written, or visual representation to a prospective franchisee or for general dissemination in the media which states or suggests a specific level or range of potential or actual sales, income, gross, or net profits."[3] To make an earnings claim to franchisees, you must provide documented evidence that is relevant to the franchisee's location, and you must provide the earnings claim when you provide the other disclosure documents.[4]

Only 25 percent of franchisors provide franchisees with earnings claims.[5] Franchisors offer several reasons for not providing earnings claims. One is that, in some locations, franchisors can be held liable if they give improper information in earnings claims. Another is that, once used in a dispute, earnings claims often become a focal point for subsequent legal conflict. Still another reason not to offer earnings claims is that the franchisor considers earnings information to be a trade secret and does not want to undermine the value of that information by disclosing it.[6]

Despite these reasons for not offering earnings claims, most franchisors find them to be very useful in attracting franchisees. For instance, educational training franchisor ComputerTots® found that its franchisees viewed its earnings claims as a signal of the company's trustworthiness and that providing an earnings claim helps attract franchisees.

It is easy to see why. For many franchisors, earnings claims demonstrate that the franchise system is a very good investment. Take, for example, the earnings claim for Abra Auto Body & Glass, a collision-repair franchise out of Brooklyn Center, Minnesota. The document shows that the average franchisee in the system earns $137,277 per year before manager bonus and income taxes, and that the average initial investment in the franchise is $326,100. Therefore, the return on investment in this franchise is more than 41 percent, including the franchisee's salary.[7] That's a pretty good return, and the evidence of it is persuasive in selling franchises.

An Effective Franchise Sales Force

Offering a proven system that makes money for franchisees is not enough to recruit franchisees. You also must have an effective franchise sales force that knows how to sell franchises. Therefore, when you decide to franchise, you have to commit yourself to a change in your business. Rather than selling the product or service that you had previously provided to your customer, you have to sell your business opportunity. Selling franchises means that you need to have sales-people with experience selling big-ticket items. These salespeople have to know how to qualify prospects and convert them to your business. They need to overcome objections and show prospective franchisees the benefits of your system over alternative business opportunities.

You also need to support your franchise sales force with the right documentary materials on the franchise system, whether this material is a prototype outlet, an earnings claim form, or other materials. Furthermore, your franchise sales force needs the right incentives to sell franchises, with a commission schedule that motivates them, without giving them too much of an inclination to bring in franchisees that are unqualified or that the system cannot support.

Stop! Don't Do It!

1. Don't try to recruit franchisees if you don't have a valuable operating system and demonstrated evidence of franchisee profitability.

2. Don't forget to create a franchise sales force that knows how to sell business opportunities, and that has the information and incentives to do so.

Selecting Franchisees

Franchisors often fail because they select the wrong franchisees. Therefore, building a successful franchise system isn't just about recruiting franchisees. It is also about identifying the right franchisees—people with the right background, skills, abilities, and attitudes—for your system.

Selecting the right franchisees for a business is a lot harder than selecting the right employees. Most employment contracts involve employment at will, making it relatively easy to lay someone off if he or she doesn't work out as an employee. But franchising involves signing a contract for many years. If you pick the wrong franchisees, you are stuck with them for a while. Thus, identifying the right franchisees is crucial, and you should spend a lot of time and effort on it.

Large, established franchisors such as McDonald's have a big advantage in selecting franchisees. A very effective screening mechanism is to have prospective franchisees work in an outlet for a period of time before becoming a franchisee. McDonald's reputation lets it impose this requirement on its potential franchisees. But you—and most new franchisors like you—must select franchisees without the opportunity to observe them working in an outlet for a while. To do this effectively, you need to employ some selection criteria. The key ones that most franchisors use are industry experience, startup experience, net worth requirements, and psychological tests.

Industry Experience

One criterion used by franchisors to select franchisees is industry experience. Although 70 percent of franchisees buy businesses in industries other than those that they worked in before,[8] some franchisors do not want inexperienced franchisees. These franchisors look for information in their potential franchisees' applications that indicate industry experience. For instance, DuctBusters®, a Clearwater, Florida, franchisor of air-duct-cleaning businesses, considers industry experience to be very important in the selection of franchisees and sells only to people in the air-conditioning contracting business.[9]

When you start franchising, you probably want to look for franchisees with industry experience. Research shows that selecting franchisees with that experience is very beneficial when the franchise system is new.[10] Experienced franchisees provide the new chain with management skills that it might be lacking. Moreover, they provide knowledge of the market that helps to sell products effectively to customers.

It is interesting to note that industry experience is a much more important selection criterion for franchisors than education, which is often an important criterion in selecting managers at companies. Few franchisors consider the formal education of prospective franchisees to be very important in selecting franchisees. In fact, many franchisors, such as Minuteman Press® of Farmingdale, New York, report that formal education is completely unimportant in selecting their franchisees.[11] As a franchisor, you probably don't want to worry very much about the formal education of your prospective franchisees.

Startup Experience

Another important criterion used by some franchisors to select franchisees is entrepreneurial experience. Many franchisors do not want to sell franchises to people with startup experience, arguing that experienced entrepreneurs are more difficult to train. In fact, one study showed that the probability of becoming a franchisee is 6.5 percent lower if the potential franchisee owned a business before.[12] Therefore, most people who buy franchises do not have current or past entrepreneurial experience. And you probably don't want to make startup experience a requirement for becoming a franchisee in your system.

Net Worth Requirements

The franchisee's initial investment—the amount of money that he or she needs to invest to create the franchised outlet, including the cost of leases, equipment, and inventory to operate a business—can range from around $100,000 to as high as several million dollars. For instance, the initial investment of a franchisee in Doubletree® Hotels ranges from $7 million to $40 million. In contrast, a franchisee needs to invest only between $70,000 and $150,000 to open a Snappy Tomato Pizza franchise.[13]

The high levels of initial investment required to buy many franchises make franchisee net worth a third important criterion used by some franchisors to select franchisees. For example, Country Inns and Suites®, a lodging franchisor, considers franchisee net worth to be a very important criterion for selection and has a minimum net worth requirement for its franchisees.[14]

Net worth is an important selection criterion. The cost of opening a franchised outlet greatly exceeds the cost of establishing a new independent business. Some estimates in the restaurant industry are that franchised outlets require three to four times the initial capitalization of nonfranchised outlets.[15] Research shows that franchisees with low net worth tend to perform poorly. Therefore, selecting franchisees with more capital available to them is a good idea.

In addition, having high levels of up-front investment and selecting only those people who can make that investment serves as a useful screen to weed out poor outlet operators. Only those people with good skills and abilities as franchisees are willing to make high investments in their capabilities as entrepreneurs. Therefore, having high levels of investment and selecting based on franchisee net worth are effective in finding good outlet operators.

Psychological Attributes

A final selection criterion used by many franchisors to select franchisees is assessment of the franchisee's psychological makeup. For instance, Lawn Doctor, a lawn care franchisor out of Holmdel, New Jersey, considers a personal interview with prospective franchises to be a very important qualifying criterion.[16] Dunkin Donuts, a donut franchisor out of Randolph, Massachusetts, goes even further, using a psychological profile to select its franchisees.[17]

Psychological profiling is useful as a selection criterion for franchisors for several reasons. Franchisees need to have the right motivations to be successful. In addition, characteristics such as tenacity and maturity help them to manage employees and serve customers. Because of the nature of the franchise system, the franchisee needs to be a team player. This makes the ability to get along with others an important characteristic on which to select franchisees. Therefore, when you start looking for your franchisees, you probably want to employ some sort of psychological profile to select between prospective applicants.

Stages of Screening

Many franchisors use several stages of screening to select the right franchisees for their systems. To save time and money, they use initial Internet surveys to prequalify potential franchisees before franchisor sales personnel contact them. For example, Ben & Jerry's® uses a ten-question Internet survey that asks about the person's net worth, industry experience, and willingness to serve as an owner operator. Only prospective franchisees whose answers to the survey meet the Ben & Jerry's franchisee profile are contacted by the franchisor for further discussion.

Many franchisors also divide the in-person part of the selection process into several stages. For instance, at Damon's® Grill, a casual dining franchisor out of Columbus, Ohio, the first meeting with prospective franchisees is spent describing the franchisor and its support services, as well as the roles and responsibilities of the franchisee. A subsequent meeting occurs at the franchisor's home office, where the prospective franchisee meets with senior executives of the company.

When you start franchising, you should consider using staged screening; it is likely to save you time and money, while still helping you to find excellent franchisees.

Stop! Don't Do It!

1. Don't select franchisees without some sort of selection criteria; net worth requirements, industry experience, start-up experience, and psychological testing are important ones used by many franchisors.

2. Don't try to talk to all potential franchisees; set up an initial screening mechanism to weed out unpromising franchisees before talking to them.

Managing Franchisees

Managing franchisees is an important part of what it takes to be a successful franchisor. Most books on franchising are full of large amounts of pseudopsychological mumbo-jumbo about things that you can supposedly do to build strong positive relationships with your franchisees. But the reality is that you will not be able to make your franchisees your best friends—and that should not be your goal. All the marriage analogies of franchising aside, your goals and those of your franchisees are not the same. There is bound to be some conflict between you. Managing franchisees is never easy, but four basic activities go a long way toward making that process more effective: minimizing conflict, generating value, communicating clearly, and controlling carefully.

Minimizing Conflicts

Let's face it: As a franchisor, you have different goals than your franchisees. As Chapter 3, "The Disadvantages of Franchising," pointed out, your franchisees are legally independent businesses whose objective is to maximize profits net of royalties at their outlets. Your objective is to maximize sales across your entire franchise system. Those goals come into conflict over such issues as the density of outlets in an area and collective action among outlet operators.

Your best bet for getting along well with your franchisees is to look carefully at the sources of conflict that are fundamental to franchising (outlined largely in Chapter 3) and minimize them. The fewer sources of conflict that you have, the better you and your franchisees will get along. If you can find a way to provide additional services to franchisees over time, leading them not to see franchising as an obsolescing bargain, you will be better off. Similarly, if you can set up your system to minimize the need for collective action among franchisees, your relationship with your franchisees will be better. The fewer the sources of goal conflict are between you and your franchisees, the less likely it will be that you or your franchisees will engage in some sort of irrational action out of frustration over conflict that undermines the ability of both of you to make money from franchising.

Generating Value

Even though conflict with franchisees is inevitable, it doesn't mean that it has to undermine your franchise system. Many franchisees in successful systems adopt the attitude that they might not agree with the actions of their franchisors, but they are willing to work with them because they make good money from their participation in the franchise system. People are willing to put up with a fair amount of goal conflict if doing so is financially beneficial to them.

This is one reason why it is very important for you to create a franchise system that generates ongoing financial returns to your franchisees. As earlier chapters pointed out, franchisees often refrain from behavior that would hurt the franchise system because they don't want to be terminated from a franchise system from which they earn significant profits. By setting up a franchise system that is profitable for franchisees in the first place, by investing in monitoring franchisees, by coming up with new products and services, and by building your brand name, you can provide your franchisees with a stream of profits that is better than what they can achieve outside the system. If that is the case, they might complain that they don't like everything that you do, but it doesn't matter—they will conform to the rules of the system and make money for themselves and for you.

Communicating Clearly

Another piece of managing franchisees effectively is communicating clearly with them. Clear communication begins when you first begin selling the franchise. If you are fair and honest with your franchisees about what benefits they will derive from entering into a franchise agreement with you, they will be less likely to be upset by the outcomes they encounter later. As long as their results are consistent with what you told them they would be in the first place, their expectations will be met.

You also want to be clear and precise in your franchise agreement. Spell out exactly what your franchisees' obligations are to the system. For example, if you want your franchisees to spend 5 percent of their sales on local advertising, tell them that in the franchise agreement. Don't tell them that local advertising expenditures are at the discretion of the franchisor, get them to buy into the system, and then tell them the magic number for advertising is 5 percent. You might scare off a few prospective franchisees by telling them up front what the numbers for your franchise system actually are, but you will save all of you a lot of grief by making sure everyone is clear on expectations. Disputes between franchisees and franchisors tend to occur when franchisees think that the policies of the system are one thing and you tell them later that they are another.

Over time, make sure that you maintain open and honest communication with your franchisees. Your franchisees likely will disagree with your actions when their goals diverge from yours, but they will be better able to accept those actions if you explain them than if you don't. For example, suppose your franchise agreement allows you to sell your frozen coffee drinks through supermarkets as well as through your franchise outlets. You might think that you are avoiding conflict by shipping the coffee to local supermarkets without getting into a big discussion with your franchisees over this decision. However, your franchisees are likely to get more upset by this action than if you remind them of what your arrangement with them is; tell them you are selling frozen coffee through the supermarkets; and discuss the effect that this decision is going to have on them.

Controlling Carefully

The last piece of the process of managing franchisees is to control what they can do very carefully. Managing franchisees largely involves managing their adherence to the terms of the franchise agreement that you signed with them. As was described earlier, you need to clearly state your franchisees' obligations and your remedies for their failure to meet these obligations in the contracts that you sign with them.

But that is only half of the process. You also need to monitor your franchisees to determine whether they are adhering to the terms of your franchise agreement. You need to send your franchise consultants to check on franchisees and conduct field audits of their operations, perhaps not when you first establish your franchise system and it is very small, but certainly when it has begun to grow. Using quality audits with scores that go toward evaluating franchisee eligibility for additional outlets, as well as toward possible termination for noncompliance, is a big part of ensuring that franchisees adhere to their obligations to the franchise system.

Also, you need to make sure that you treat all of your franchisees similarly with the control mechanisms that you employ. Not only will you run into trouble with franchise discrimination laws if you, say, audit nearby franchises much more often than the ones far away from headquarters, but your franchisees also will be much more likely to free-ride and engage in other problematic activities if they think that you aren't going to check on their behavior. When you set up your franchise system, make sure that you have a plan for how to monitor and audit your franchisees so that whatever approach you use treats all your franchisees fairly.

Stop! Don't Do It!

1. Don't create too many areas of goal conflict with your franchisees.

2. Don't try to manage franchisees unless you make the system profitable for them; controlling franchisees that don't benefit from a system is a losing battle.

3. Don't avoid conflict by being vague about franchisee obligations; state them clearly in your franchise contract and your communications with franchisees.

Questions to Ask Yourself

1. Why would people buy my franchise instead of doing this business themselves?

2. Why would people buy my franchise instead of buying from a different franchisor?

3. Am I willing and able to create a franchising sales force?

4. Do I have a template for selecting motivated and skilled franchisees?

5. Do I know how to create value, minimize conflict, communicate effectively, and control carefully when I manage my franchisees?

Summary

This chapter offered specific information to help you determine how to recruit, select, and manage franchisees. The first part of the chapter discussed how to recruit franchisees, explaining that two factors are particularly important: understanding why people buy franchises and offering them something that they want to buy, and developing a professional sales force that knows how to generate a pool of prospects and sell them on the franchise system.

People buy franchises to get access to a proven system and to make money. Therefore, to be successful, you need to offer a valuable business format, a manual to operate the business, training, ongoing assistance, and a brand name. You also need to generate a business opportunity with a profit stream that exceeds what franchisees would earn in alternative employment and document that information for franchisees through a uniform franchise offering circular.

To sell franchises effectively, you need to create a sales force with experience selling business opportunities. That sales force needs to know how to qualify its prospects, overcome objections, and close sales. You also need to support this sales force with the right documentary information and incentives.

Franchisors often fail because they select the wrong franchisees. Selecting franchisees is harder than selecting employees because employees can be terminated much more easily than franchisees. Effective franchisee selection criteria include industry experience, start-up experience, net worth requirements, and psychological profiling.

Managing franchisees is an important part of what it takes to be a successful franchisor. Although managing franchisees is not easy, four basic activities go a long way toward making that process more effective: minimizing the number of sources of goal conflict with franchisees, ensuring that the franchise system provides financial benefit to them, communicating clearly about their obligations, and controlling their behavior carefully.

Now that you understand all 11 rules of franchising, we turn to some thoughts about how to bring them all together, in the final chapter.

CONCLUSIONS

This book offered 11 rules for you to follow to develop a successful franchise system. Each of these rules was explained in a different chapter of the book:

1. Select the right industry.

2. Understand the advantages of franchising.

3. Pay attention to the disadvantages of franchising.

4. Make sure you have a business concept that can be franchised.

5. Adopt the right policies to manage the franchise system.

6. Find the right approach to franchisee support and assistance.

7. Develop the right strategy toward franchisee territories.

8. Price the franchises appropriately.

9. Develop the right strategy toward system expansion.

10. Understand the legal and institutional environment of franchising.

11. Recruit, select, and manage franchisees effectively.

To follow these 11 rules, you should do the things summarized here:

Rule no. 1: Select the right industry. You will be more successful if you select the right industry in which to franchise your business. The right industries for franchising are ones that involve local production and distribution in limited geographic markets. They also demand physical locations. Local market knowledge is important to performance, local management discretion is beneficial, and brand name reputation is a valuable competitive advantage. The process of creating and delivering the product or service sold to end customers must be one that can be standardized and codified. Operations tend to be labor intensive, and the effort of employees in the industry is more difficult to measure than their performance.

Rule no. 2: Understand the advantages of franchising. You will make better decisions about franchising if you understand the benefits that this business model can offer. Franchising is a very effective mechanism for selecting talented outlet operators and providing them with appropriate incentives to work hard. Franchising is an excellent mode of business if you need to obtain capital and human resources from others to permit rapid firm growth. Furthermore, franchising offers a lucrative economic model, generating financial returns at relatively low risk.

Rule no. 3: Pay attention to the disadvantages of franchising. To accurately judge whether you should franchise, you need to understand that franchising is not a panacea for all business problems and has four major drawbacks:

- Franchisors and franchisees are independent businesses with different goals that come into conflict.
- Using contracts to link franchisors with franchisees leads to transaction cost problems that do not exist within company-owned chains.
- Innovation and change initiated at headquarters are more difficult to implement with franchising than with company ownership of outlets.
- The absolute amount of profits from franchising is lower than that from operating outlets.

Rule no. 4: Make sure that you have a business concept that can be franchised. You will be more successful if you franchise a business concept that is appropriate for franchising than if you do not. Franchising works better if the business concept is based on a valuable system for serving end customers that can bear the additional costs of the franchising structure. It is also more effective if the system can be broken down into a set of operating rules that can be written down and taught to others with limited knowledge of the business. Furthermore, the business must appeal to enough potential buyers of the concept to make investing in the up-front costs of setting up a franchise system worthwhile.

Rule no. 5: Adopt the right policies to manage a franchise system effectively. Strong performance at franchising requires different policies than those used in chains of company-owned outlets because franchising is a business based on contracts between legally independent companies. One key policy is to ensure owner operation of outlets. Another is to set longer-term contracts with your franchisees, unless you do not think that you can pick winning franchisees or you think that you will need to modify your franchise operation repeatedly over time. Your success as a franchisor will also be enhanced by establishing tight controls over franchisee behavior, including detailed contract provisions outlining franchisee behavior, your termination rights, sources of franchisee supply, and requirements for exclusive dealing, as well as by providing franchisees with excess profits and an increasingly valuable brand name. Finally, your likelihood of success will be enhanced by requiring franchisees to invest a portion of their revenues in national and cooperative local advertising.

Rule no. 6: Find the right approach to franchisee support and assistance. To succeed at franchising, you need to offer the right amount of franchisee training and support—enough to provide franchisees with what they need to operate their businesses, but not more than your business can afford to provide. You will be most successful if you match the amount, timing, and location of training to industry conditions, the characteristics of your operating system, and your company's age and size. Your franchise system also will be more successful if it offers field operations evaluation and real estate assistance to franchisees, but not when the system is very young. Offering centralized services in areas in which economies of scale are strongest, such as inventory control and purchasing, will also help. Your success will be enhanced by creating communications mechanisms to link franchisees to your operation and to each other, particularly as your franchise system grows. Finally, you will be more successful if you provide franchisees with indirect financing assistance rather than financing them directly or not helping them with financing.

Rule no. 7: Develop the right strategy toward franchisee territories. Your performance as a franchisor will be enhanced if you do not rely on multiunit franchising when your franchise system is first established, unless your system needs to grow so rapidly that the beneficial effects of growth dominate the adverse effects of multiunit arrangements. Your success will be enhanced by allowing existing franchisees to expand the number of outlets in their territories and by providing franchisees with exclusive territories, as long as those territories are not so large that they allow your competitors to develop a better position in the market than you have. You also will be more successful if you adopt complementary territorial strategies and franchise policies jointly than if you develop them independently.

Rule no. 8: Price the franchises appropriately. You will be more successful if you charge the right price for your franchise system than if you over- or undercharge franchisees. The right royalty rate and franchise fee for your system depend on the nature of your industry, your system's attributes, the length of your contract term, your firm's age and size, and the value of your brand name reputation. You will not be successful if you try to capture too much of the cost of the franchise in the form of the up-front fee instead of ongoing royalties. In fact, you will be more successful with a new franchise system if you bias your compensation away from up-front fees and toward royalty rates when your system is first established. Over time, your success will allow you to raise both up-front fees and royalty rates, with royalty rates rising more slowly than up-front fees to rebalance the compensation between the two sources of revenue.

Rule no. 9: Develop the right strategy toward system expansion. You are best off operating your business for several years before you begin franchising. When you first begin to franchise, you will be more successful if you maintain the company-owned outlets that you already have and add new outlets by franchising intensively in a concentrated geographic area. When your system becomes mature, you are likely to gain by repurchasing at least some of your franchised outlets. In terms of specific outlets to franchise and own, you will be more successful if you franchise those outlets most distant from your headquarters and those located in less populated areas, and own those outlets near headquarters and in densely populated locations. You also will be best off if you own outlets in locations where there are few repeat customers and where performance is not correlated with that in other outlets. Your international expansion will be most successful if you first operate domestically for several years, building up the size of your system, saturating your market, and working out the kinks in your operating policies. When you do eventually expand overseas, your likelihood of success will increase if you use master franchising, raise your up-front franchise fees and lower your royalty rates, and franchise a greater proportion of your outlets than you do in your home market.

Rule no. 10: Understand the legal and institutional environment of franchising. To succeed you need to ensure that your franchise system conforms to the legal and institutional environment in which you operate. Federal law requires you to provide your franchisees with a standard disclosure document at least ten days before you sign a franchise agreement with them. To adhere to state laws, you must know which states regulate franchising and which do not. Because only some states regulate franchising, when you begin to franchise, you will need to decide whether to operate in regulated states as a way to signal the quality of your system or to avoid those states to keep your costs down. If you choose to sell franchises in states that require franchisor registration, you must ensure that you adhere to all of the requirements imposed by the regulatory authorities. Similarly, if you choose to sell franchises in states that have franchise relationship laws, you should charge higher royalty rates and rely more heavily on franchising than you otherwise would, unless you are operating in an industry with few repeat customers. Finally, you will be more successful if you seek certification of your franchise system from the media or by joining the franchise trade association.

Rule no. 11: Recruit, select, and manage franchisees effectively. You will be more successful if you offer franchisees a proven system that generates profits for them. Providing an earnings claims disclosure is an important way to demonstrate that your franchise system generates sufficient profits for franchisees to earn a decent return on their investment. Your success will be enhanced by hiring a franchise sales staff that knows how to sell business opportunities, and by supporting that staff with proper incentives and documentation on the franchise system. Your franchise operation will also be more successful if you develop effective criteria to select franchisees from the pool of applicants, whether those criteria are industry experience requirements, net worth requirements, or scores on psychological tests. Finally, your franchise operation will be more successful if you manage relationships with franchisees by minimizing the number of areas of franchisor-franchisee conflict, generating value for your franchisees, communicating the rules of the system clearly, and controlling franchisee behavior carefully.

A Final Comment

Of the vast numbers of companies that begin to franchise every year, only a few are very successful. Most of the entrepreneurs and managers who establish new franchise systems—more than 75 percent over 10 years and 85 percent over 17 years—end up with failed ventures and little financial returns to show for all of their effort. However, every year a small number of people start truly successful franchise systems that go public and generate tremendous riches for them and nearly everyone involved with their ventures. Although the odds of being very successful are not great, that doesn't mean that you are powerless to improve your chances of being among the small number of success stories.

As this book has explained, being a successful founder of a franchise system is much like being a good professional gambler. If you know the games where the odds are least stacked in favor of the house, and you understand the rules of the game you are playing, you can greatly improve your chances of winning. Following the rules outlined in the book will help you to set up a winning franchise system. Although this information will not guarantee your success, it will increase your odds dramatically.

NOTES

Introduction

1. R. Kaiser, "Franchise Owners Like State of Industry," *Knight Ridder Tribune Business News* (14 March 2003): 1.
2. IFA Resource Center, "How Widespread Is Franchising?", www.franchise.org/resourcectr/faq/q4.asp.
3. Calculated from data contained in Entrepreneur Magazine, "Franchise 500" (January 2004): 160-255.
4. A. Sherman, "Franchising and Licensing: Two Ways to Build Your Business" (New York: AMACOM, 1991).
5. International Franchise Association, "The Profile of Franchising," (Washington, DC: The IFA Educational Foundation, 2000).
6. P. Murphy, "A Perfect Fit: Why the Franchise Sector Is Attractive to Private Equity," *Franchise World* 35(7): 23.
7. J. Bradach, *Franchise Organizations*, (Boston: Harvard Business School Press, 1998).
8. J. Combs and D. Ketchen, "Why Do Firms Use Franchising as an Entrepreneurial Strategy? A Meta Analysis." *Journal of Management* 29, no. 3 (2003): 443–465.

Chapter 1: Is Franchising Right for Your Industry?

1. International Franchise Association, *The Profile of Franchising*, (Washington, DC: The IFA Educational Foundation, 2000).
2. J. Combs and D. Ketchen, "Why Do Firms Use Franchising as an Entrepreneurial Strategy? A Meta Analysis," *Journal of Management* 29, no. 3 (2003): 443–465.
3. S. Shane, "Why New Franchisors Succeed" (report for the Office of Advocacy, U.S. Small Business Administration, contract SBAHQ-96-0419, 1996).
4. Frandata, "Franchisor Bankruptcy Study" (Washington, DC: Frandata Corporation, 1995).
5. R. Purvin, "Franchising: Yesterday, Today, and Tomorrow," in *Franchising 101: The Complete Guide to Evaluating, Buying and Growing Your Franchise Business*, ed. A. Dugan (Chicago: Dearborn Financial Publishing, 1998).
6. Ibid.
7. Ibid.
8. W. Lasher and C. Hausman, *Small Business Franchises Made Simple* (New York: Doubleday, 1994).
9. R. Thompson, "Company Ownership vs. Franchising: Issues and Evidence," *Journal of Economic Studies* 19 (4): 31–42.
10. W. Lasher and C. Hausman, *Small Business Franchises Made Simple*. op. cit.
11. J. Love, *McDonald's: Behind the Arches* (New York: Bantam Books, 1986).
12. R. Caves and W. Murphy, "Franchising: Firms, Markets, and Intangible Assets," *Southern Economic Journal* 42, no. 4 (1976): 572–586.
13. D. Thomas and M. Seid, *Franchising for Dummies* (New York: Hungry Minds, 2000).
14. R. Thompson, "Company Ownership vs. Franchising: Issues and Evidence." op. cit.
15. F. Lafontaine and M. Slade, "Retail Contracting and Costly Monitoring: Theory and Evidence," *European Economic Review* 40 (1996): 923–932.

Chapter 2: The Advantages of Franchising

1. S. Shane, "Making New Franchise Systems Work," *Strategic Management Journal* 19, no. 7 (1998): 697–707.
2. Ibid.
3. F. Lafontaine, "Franchising vs. Corporate Ownership: The Effect on Price Dispersion," *Journal of Business Venturing* 14, no. 1 (1998): 17–34.
4. T. Bates, "Survival Patterns Among Newcomers to Franchising," *Journal of Business Venturing* 13, no. 2 (1998): 113–130.

5. A. Krueger, "Ownership, Agency, and Wages: An Examination of Franchising in the Fast Food Industry," *Quarterly Journal of Economics* (1991): 76–101.

6. N. Lutz, "Ownership Rights and Incentives in Franchising," *Journal of Corporate Finance* 2 (1995): 103–131.

7. S. Spinelli, R. Rosenberg, and S. Birley, *Franchising: Pathway to Wealth Creation* (Upper Saddle River, NJ: Financial Times Prentice Hall, 2004).

8. "Franchise 500," *Entrepreneur Magazine* (January 2004): 160-225.

9. S. Norton, "Is Franchising a Capital Structure Issue?" *Journal of Corporate Finance* 2 (1995): 75–101.

10. R. Dant, "Motivations for Franchising: Rhetoric versus Reality," *International Small Business Journal* (14): 10–32.

11. P. Birkland, *Franchising Dreams* (Chicago: University of Chicago Press, 2002).

12. Ibid.

13. E. Keup, *Franchise Bible* (Grants Pass, OR: Oasis Press, 1995).

14. J. Bradach, "Using the Plural Form in the Management of Restaurant Chains," *Administrative Science Quarterly* 42 (1997): 276–303.

15. F. Lafontaine, "Franchising Survey" (Carnegie Mellon University, 1989).

16. P. Murphy, "A Perfect Fit: Why the Franchise Sector Is Attractive to Private Equity," *Franchise World* 35(7) (2003): 23.

17. Ibid.

Chapter 3: The Disadvantages of Franchising

1. F. Lafontaine, "Franchising vs. Corporate Ownership: The Effect on Price Dispersion, *Journal of Business Venturing* 14(1) (1998): 17–34.

2. P. Birkland, *Franchising Dreams* (Chicago: University of Chicago Press, 1998).

3. K. Kanouse, *Guide to Understanding an Offering Circular and Negotiating a Franchise Agreement*, (Chapel Hill: Professional Press, 1995).

4. B. Klein, and L. Saft, "The Law and Economics of Franchise Tying Contracts," *Journal of Law and Economics* 28 (1985): 345–361.

5. International Franchise Association. *The Profile of Franchising* (Washington, D.C.: The IFA Educational Foundation, 2000).

6. J. Bercovitz, "An Analysis of the Contract Provisions in Business Format Franchisee Agreements," *Working Paper* (Berkeley, CA: University of California at Berkeley, 1996).

7. G. Hadfield, "Problematic Relations: Franchising and the Law of Incomplete Contracts," *Stanford Law Review* 42 (1990): 927–992.

8. P. Azoulay and S. Shane, "Entrepreneurs, Contracts, and the Failure of Young Firms," *Management Science* 47(3) (2001): 337–358.

9. J. Brickley and F. Dark, "The Choice of Organizational Form: The Case of Franchising," *Journal of Financial Economics* 18 (1987): 401–420.

10. K. Arrow, "Economic Welfare and the Allocation of Resources for Inventions," in R. Nelson (ed.), *The Rate and Direction of Inventive Activity* (Princeton, NJ: Princeton University Press, 1962).

11. S. Spinelli, R. Rosenberg, and S. Birley, *Franchising: Pathway to Wealth Creation* (Upper Saddle River, NJ: Financial Times Prentice Hall, 2004).

12. A. Spector, "Chain Technology Evolves with Updated Franchisor Contracts, Franchisee Incentives," *Nation's Restaurant News* 37 (49) (2003): 34.

13. J. Bradach, *Franchise Organizations* (Boston: Harvard Business School Press, 1998).

14. E. Darr, L. Argote, and D. Epple, "The Acquisition, Transfer, and Depreciation of Knowledge in Service Organizations: Productivity in Franchises," *Management Science* 41(11) (1995): 1750–1762.

15. E. Smith, "Franchise Fray," *Akron Beacon Journal* 17 May (2004): D1–D2.

16. Calculated from data contained in R. Bond, *How Much Can I Make?* (Oakland, CA: Sourcebook Publications, 1997); and R. Bond's *Bond's Franchise Guide* (Oakland, CA: Sourcebook Publications: 2004).

Chapter 4: What Business Concepts Can Be Franchised?

1. T. Reeves, "Microbiology and Business," *Franchising World* 35(5) (2003): 72.

2. D. Thomas and M. Seid, *Franchising for Dummies* (New York: Hungry Minds, 2000).

3. R. Bond, *Bond's Franchise Guide* (Oakland, CA: Sourcebook Publications, 2004).

4. Ibid.

Chapter 5: Key Franchising Policies

1. S. Shane, "Making New Franchise Systems Work," *Strategic Management Journal* 19(7) (1998): 697–707.

2. International Franchise Association, *The Profile of Franchising* (Washington, DC: The IFA Educational Foundation, 2000).

3. R. Bond, *Bond's Franchise Guide* (Oakland, CA: Sourcebook Publications, 2004).

4. Ibid.

5. J. Love, *Franchising: Behind the Arches* (New York: Bantam Books, 1986).

6. J. Brickley and F. Dark, "The Choice of Organizational Form: The Case of Franchising," *Journal of Financial Economics* (18) (1987): 401–420.

7. A. Dnes, "'Unfair' Contractual Practices and Hostages in Franchise Contracts," *Journal of International and Theoretical Economics* (148) (1992): 484–504.
8. S. Michael and H. Moore, "Returns to Franchising," *Journal of Corporate Finance* (2) (1995): 133–155.
9. International Franchise Association, *The Profile of Franchising* (Washington, DC: The IFA Educational Foundation, 2000).
10. Ibid.
11. R. Bond, *Bond's Franchise Guide*. op.cit.
12. S. Shane and C. Spell, "Factors for New Franchise Success," *Sloan Management Review* (39)(3) (1998): 43–50.
13. R. Bond, *Bond's Franchise Guide*. op.cit.
14. International Franchise Association, *The Profile of Franchising*. op.cit.
15. Ibid.
16. A. Sherman, *Franchising and Licensing: Two Ways to Build Your Business* (New York: AMACOM, 1991).
17. R. Bond, *Bond's Franchise Guide*. op.cit.
18. Ibid.
19. R. Dant and P. Berger, "Modeling Cooperative Advertising Decisions in Franchising," *Journal of the Operational Research Society* (47) (1996): 1120–1136.
20. J. Beales and T. Muris, "The Foundations of Franchise Regulation: Issues and Evidence," *Journal of Corporate Finance* (2) (1995): 157–197.

Chapter 6: Franchisee Support and Assistance

1. East Coast Custard, *Key Questions and Answers*, unpublished, 2002.
2. R. Bond, *Bond's Franchise Guide* (Oakland, CA: Sourcebook Publications, 2004).
3. Ibid.
4. S. Shane and C. Spell, "Factors for New Franchise Success, *Sloan Management Review* 39(3) (1998): 43–50.
5. R. Bond, *Bond's Franchise Guide*. op.cit.
6. S. Shane and C. Spell, C, "Factors for New Franchise Success." op.cit.
7. R. Bond, *Bond's Franchise Guide*. op.cit.
8. S. Shane, "Making New Franchise Systems Work," *Strategic Management Journal* (19) (1998): 697–707.
9. R. Bond, *Bond's Franchise Guide*. op.cit.
10. Ibid.
11. International Franchise Association, *The Profile of Franchising* (Washington, DC: The IFA Educational Foundation, 2000).

Chapter 7: Territorial Strategies

1. R. Hoffman and J. Preble, "Franchising: Selecting a Strategy for Rapid Growth," *Long Range Planning* 24(4) (1991): 74–85.
2. S. Shane, "Making New Franchise Systems Work," *Strategic Management Journal* 19 (1998): 697–707.
3. J. Love, *Franchising: Behind the Arches* (New York: Bantam Books, 1986).
4. International Franchise Association, *The Profile of Franchising* (Washington, DC: The IFA Educational Foundation, 2000).
5. R. Bond, *Bond's Franchise Guide* (Oakland, CA: Sourcebook Publications, 2004).
6. P. Kaufmann, "The Impact of Managerial Performance Decay on Franchisors' Store Allocation Strategies," *Journal of Marketing Channels* 1(4) (1992): 51–79.
7. Ibid.
8. R. Bond, *Bond's Franchise Guide*. op.cit.
9. Ibid.
10. M. Tomzack, *Tips & Traps When Buying a Franchise* (Oakland, CA: Sourcebook Publications, 1999).
11. P. Kaufmann and F. Lafontaine, "Costs of Control: The Source of Economic Rents for McDonald's Franchisees," *The Journal of Law and Economics* 37(2) (1994): 417–453.
12. International Franchise Association, *The Profile of Franchising*. op.cit.
13. J. Tannenbaum, "Focus on Franchising: LaFalce Gains Allies in House to Halt Franchise Abuses," *Wall Street Journal* (July 9, 1993): B2.
14. International Franchise Association, *The Profile of Franchising*. op.cit.
15. F. Mathewson and R. Winter, "Territorial Restrictions in Franchise Contracts," *Economic Inquiry* 32 (1985): 181–192.
16. Ibid.

Chapter 8: Pricing Franchises

1. D. Foster, *The Complete Franchise Book* (Rocklin, CA: Prima Publishing, 1984).
2. International Franchise Association, *The Profile of Franchising* (Washington, DC: The IFA Educational Foundation, 2000).
3. D. Foster, *The Complete Franchise Book*. op.cit.
4. F. Lafontaine, "How and Why Franchisors Do What They Do: A Survey Report," *Proceedings of the 6th Conference of the Society of Franchising* (1991), P. Kaufmann (ed.).
5. F. Lafontaine and K. Shaw, "The Dynamics of Franchise Contracting: Evidence from Panel Data," *Journal of Political Economy* 107(5) (1999): 1041–1080.
6. J. Love, *Franchising: Behind the Arches* (New York: Bantam Books, 1986).

7. International Franchise Association, *The Profile of Franchising* (Washington, DC: The IFA Educational Foundation, 2000).

8. R. Caves and W. Murphy, "Franchising: Firms, Markets, and Intangible Assets," *Southern Economic Journal* 42(4) (1976): 572–586.

9. R. Bond, *Bond's Franchise Guide* (Oakland, CA: Sourcebook Publications, 2004).

10. Ibid.

11. F. Lafontaine, "Contractual Arrangements as Signaling Devices: Evidence from Franchising," *Journal of Law, Economics, and Organization* 9(2) (1993): 256–289.

12. J. Love, *Franchising: Behind the Arches*. op.cit.

13. R. Rao and S. Srinivasan, "Why Are Royalty Rates Higher in Service-Type Franchises?" *Journal of Economics and Management Strategy* 4(1) (1995): 7–31.

14. International Franchise Association, *The Profile of Franchising*. op.cit.

Chapter 9: Expansion Strategies

1. F. Lafontaine and K. Shaw, "Franchising Growth and Franchisor Entry and Exit in the U.S. Market: Myth and Reality," *Journal of Business Venturing* 13(2) (1998): 95–112.

2. R. Bond, *Bond's Franchise Guide* (Oakland, CA: Sourcebook Publications, 2004)

3. R. Bond, *The Sourcebook of Franchise Opportunities*, (Homewood, IL: Irwin, 1989).

4. B. Cline, *Franchising* (Toronto: Praeger, 1989).

5. R. Dant, P. Kaufmann, and R. Robicheaux, "Changes in the Mix of Company-Owned and Franchised Outlets: Ownership Redirection Revisited," paper presented at the 12th Annual Society of Franchising Conference, Las Vegas, NV (March 7–8, 1998).

6. R. Bond, *Bond's Franchise Guide*. op.cit.

7. M. Tomzack, *Tips & Traps When Buying a Franchise* (Oakland, CA: Sourcebook Publications, 1999).

8. E. Gal-Or, "Maintaining Quality Standards in Franchise Chains," *Management Science* 41(11) (1995): 1774–1792.

9. R. Bond, *Bond's Franchise Guide*. op.cit.

10. P. Kaufmann and V. Rangan, "Model of Franchisor Market Penetration in an Area of Dominant Influence," in L. Pellegrini and S. Reddy (eds.) *Retail and Marketing Channels* (London: Routledge, 1992): 163–177.

11. J. Forero, "Columbians Urged to Drink More and Better Coffee (Their Own)," *New York Times* (May 29, 2004): B1,14.

12. Ibid.

13. L. Schwartz, *International Expansion by U.S. Franchisors* (New York: International Franchising Association Educational Foundation, 1996).

14. Ibid.

15. J. Preble, "Global Expansion: The Case of U.S. Fast-Food Franchisors," *Journal of Global Marketing* 6(1/2) (1992): 185–205.

16. L. Schwartz, *International Expansion*. op.cit.

17. K. Fladmoe-Linquist and L. Jacque, "To Own or to Franchise? The International Control Decision for Service Companies," *Journal of Applied Corporate Finance* 9(3) (1996): 98–108.

18. Ibid.

19. Ibid.

Chapter 10: The Legal and Institutional Environment for Franchising

1. A. Sherman, *Franchising and Licensing: Two Ways to Build Your Business* (New York: AMACOM, 1991).

2. D. Kaufmann, "An Introduction to Franchising and Franchise Law," *Prepared for Franchising: Business and Legal Issues Program*, New York State Bar Association, New York (February 26, 1992).

3. A. Sherman, *Franchising and Licensing*. op.cit.

4. C. Modell, "Before You Start Selling Franchises—a Legal Checklist for New Franchisors," *Franchising World* 34(4) (2002): 38–9.

5. R. Emerson, "Franchise Contract Clauses and the Franchisor's Duty of Care Toward Its Franchisees," *North Carolina Law Review* (72) (1994): 905–965.

6. International Franchise Association, *The Profile of Franchising* (Washington, DC: The IFA Educational Foundation, 2000).

7. R. Bond, *Bond's Franchise Guide* (Oakland, CA: Sourcebook Publications, 2004).

8. S. Shane and C. Spell, "Factors for New Franchise Success," *Sloan Management Review* 39(3) (1998): 43–50.

9. A. Caffey, *Franchises & Business Opportunities: How to Find, Buy, and Operate a Successful Business* (New York: Entrepreneur Press, 2002).

10. J. Brickley, "Royalty Rates and Up Front Fees in Share Contracts: Evidence from Franchising," *Journal of Law, Economics, and Organization* 18(2) (2002): 511–535.

11. S. Shane and M. Foo, "New Firm Survival: Institutional Explanations for New Franchisor Mortality," *Management Science* 45(2) (1999): 142–159.

12. J. Brickley, F. Dark, and M. Weisbach, "The Economic Effects of Franchise Termination Laws," *Journal of Law and Economics* (34) (1991): 101–132.

13. International Franchise Association, *Membership Application* (Washington, DC: International Franchise Association, 0.2, 1994).

14. Ibid.

15. R. Barkoff, "Government Regulation of the Franchise Relationship in the United States," *Paper presented to the Committee on International Franchising (Committee X) Section on Business Law,* International Bar Association Annual Meeting, New Orleans, LA: October 10, 1993, 10–15.

16. S. Shane, *Why New Franchisors Succeed,* (Report for the Office of Advocacy, U.S. Small Business Administration, contract SBAHQ-96-0419, 1996).

Chapter 11: Recruiting, Selecting, and Managing Franchisees

1. J. Stanworth and D. Purdy, *The Blenheim/University of Westminster Franchise Survey: Spring 1993* (University of Westminster Press, Special Studies Series 1, 1993).

2. P. Kaufmann and F. Lafontaine, "Costs of Control: The Source of Economic Rents for McDonald's Franchisees," *Journal of Law and Economics* (37) (1994): 417–452.

3. 44 Federal Register 49982.

4. A. Sherman, *Franchising and Licensing: Two Ways to Build Your Business* (New York: AMACOM, 1991).

5. International Franchise Association, *The Profile of Franchising* (Washington, DC: The IFA Educational Foundation, 2000).

6. D. Thomas and M. Seid, *Franchising for Dummies* (New York: Hungry Minds, 2000).

7. Calculated from data in R. Bond's *How Much Can I Make?* (Oakland, CA: Sourcebook Publications, 1997); and *Bond's Franchise Guide* (Oakland, CA: Sourcebook Publications, 2004).

8. P. Kaufmann, "Franchising and the Choice of Self-Employment," *Journal of Business Venturing* (14) (1999): 345–362.

9. R. Bond, *Bond's Franchise Guide.* op.cit.

10. S. Shane, "Making New Franchise Systems Work," *Strategic Management Journal* (19) (1998): 697–707.

11. R. Bond, *Bond's Franchise Guide.* op.cit.

12. D. Williams, Why Do Entrepreneurs Become Franchisees? An Empirical Analysis of Organizational Choice," *Journal of Business Venturing* (14) (1998): 103–124.

13. R. Bond, *Bond's Franchise Guide.* op.cit.

14. Ibid.

15. D. Williams, "Why Do Entrepreneurs Become Franchisees? An Empirical Analysis of Organizational Choice," op.cit.

16. R. Bond, *Bond's Franchise Guide.* op.cit.

17. Ibid.

INDEX